FOR A HOUSE MADE OF STONE

FOR A HOUSE MADE OF STONE

Gina's Story

Gina French
with Andrew Crofts

Author's Note:
In order to protect my son, Paul Donald and Michael are pseudonyms.
Other names have also been changed to protect the privacy
of the individuals involved.

First published in 2006 by Vision,
a division of Satin Publications Ltd.
101 Southwark Street
London SE1 0JF
UK
info@visionpaperbacks.co.uk
www.visionpaperbacks.co.uk
Publisher: Sheena Dewan

A catalogue record for this book is available from the British Library.

HB ISBN: 1-904132-79-0
Export PB ISBN: 1-904132-80-4

2 4 6 8 10 9 7 5 3 1

Cover and text design by ok?design
Printed and bound in the UK by
Mackays of Chatham Ltd, Chatham, Kent

CONTENTS

PROLOGUE

I no longer believe they'll hang me, but I know there's a possibility they'll lock me up for the rest of my life and I'll never be able to cuddle my children again, or go down to the river to help my mother with the family washing.

Sitting in my cell in England the night before my trial starts, I can't sleep and so I'm writing; page after page of my neat unjoined-up writing pouring onto the lined paper. I want to get out everything that's inside my head and heart, to stop them both from aching so. There have been so many things I've kept quiet about, believing I should be ashamed, or perhaps just discreet, but I don't want to hold them all inside my brain any more. I don't think anyone should be made to feel ashamed of the things they choose to do, if they choose for the right reasons.

I want to explain how it all happened, how I came to travel so far and end up in so much trouble when so many people along the way thought things would turn out differently for me. People read about my story in the English papers and made their judgements on the lurid headlines. Many of those men from around the world who knew me when I was working in the bar in Manila showed me great kindness and took an interest in how I'd come to be there with them in their hotel rooms, but I doubt they could really picture the childhood I was describing to them, or understand what life was like for my family when there was no one sending home money. The local newspaper journalists in England who wrote the headline phrases like 'killer wife' and 'Filipino ex-vice girl' couldn't be expected to understand the stranger in their midst with her different looks, different language, different tastes in food and different past.

I don't know what will happen tomorrow, when people I've never met will decide whether or not I am a bad person who should go to jail for life, but at least I'm sorting out in my mind everything that has led me to this sleepless night.

CHAPTER ONE

A Mountain Childhood

'Mama,' I said, 'where do problems come from? How can I get one?'

'Oh, Gina,' she tutted, continuing to work, scrubbing at the laundry in the foaming waters of the river as she talked, 'don't ask me about problems. One day you'll be coming to me asking how to get rid of them.'

I puzzled over her words but couldn't make sense of them. As a small child, living in the mountains with my family at the beginning of the 1970s, life seemed so simple and pleasant. I was born in 1973, but nothing much had changed for families like mine in hundreds of years. How could life ever be a problem? The sun shone most of the time, while the tropical rain showers and sea breezes kept us cool during the day. The lush, green land that we farmed as a family provided a constant supply of fruit, vegetables and rice for us to eat ourselves and sell the surplus in the market. We had our own carabaw (water buffalo) for carrying heavy loads, and flocks of chickens and ducks clucked and squawked around the house, producing eggs and meat. I had no idea how hard it was for my parents just to keep us all alive, or why adults always talked about their 'problems'.

Sometimes we would lose a chicken or two to the dragon-like lizards that emerged from the jungle in search of easy prey. They stood perfectly still for hours on end, camouflaged against the foliage, until the moment they pounced, when they moved so fast you could barely see them. Now and then our father would even the score by killing one of the dragons with his machete and Mum would cook that instead – their meat always tasted very like the chickens they'd killed.

There was always just enough to eat, even if there were never any sweets, which were the things we children constantly craved. It was a simple diet, which kept us all healthy most of the time. Compared to most people, of course, we had almost nothing; we were simply fortunate we didn't live in a part of the world that suffered regular droughts or floods or we would have starved. We were kept alive by the grace of the nature we lived amongst.

Mainly our diet was fish and green vegetables. Once a week, at the weekend, Mum might try to buy meat, mainly pork. If she couldn't afford that we would kill one of the chickens or ducks. The poultry (and lizards) were the only sort of regular meat we could afford and they had to be rationed carefully. Mum would never kill more than one bird and would divide it up to feed all of us, including her and Dad. In the West one bird wouldn't even make a single meal for so many people, but she was clever at cutting it into the smallest pieces possible, stripping the bones clean and leaving nothing to waste, sharing it out fairly.

Sometimes, if we were having a celebration like a birthday, we'd eat one of the dogs; there was no room for sentimentality about any of the animals. Dogs tasted good, but I don't think I would be able to bring myself to eat one now. Sometimes at the weekends there would be cockfights to watch, with all the grown-ups shouting and screaming with excitement as the blood and feathers flew, laying bets and encouraging the birds to attack one another more viciously until one would strut away from its destroyed opponent, battered but victorious. The grown-ups said the spectacle helped them forget their problems for a short while.

To make a little extra money our mother took bananas, pineapples, guavas, yams and coconuts into the town to sell. She would return with dried fish, which would last us for days, but never with sweets or pretty clothes or shoes. That was okay, we understood. Life was still good, despite these little disappointments. We seldom had fresh fish because we had no means of keeping it cool so we would have to eat it all the same day it was bought, which would mean no more protein for the rest of the week. One day one of the cats stole our week's supply of dried fish and Mum killed it in an explosion of anger.

'We'll have to eat it,' she told us as we watched her skinning the bony corpse, 'otherwise we'll get a year of bad luck.'

I couldn't see how our luck could get much worse than having to eat cat meat; it tasted disgusting.

The Philippines is made up of around 7,000 islands, although only about 700 of them are inhabited. The two biggest are Luzon and Mindanao. We lived on Luzon, which is where the capital, Manila, is. I heard tales about this distant city with all its opportunities and dangers, but I couldn't imagine what it might look like.

I dare say anyone looking at my idyllic childhood from the Western world would have seen that both my parents had more than their fair share of hardships and problems to contend with. But to me in my first five years, running barefoot around the old wooden house and into the fertile jungles outside, play-acting at helping with the chores, there didn't seem to be anything wrong with our lives. We ate and we slept and we worked to keep the house clean and food on the table; it seemed more than enough. Other relatives, including my grandparents, aunts, uncles and cousins, lived in neighbouring houses so there was always someone to talk to or play with, all of us sharing the same history and facing the same future.

★

I only gradually learned the difficulties my parents faced, and of the bitterness and division amongst the elders of my family. My parents, Norma and Emiliano, met when Mum was 14. She'd had to leave school without learning to read or write in order to help the men in her family. Her life had been a struggle ever since and she faced up to it without complaint. Papa was only 16 but the extra two years of schooling made all the difference between them. Dad could at least read and write, which Mum never could.

Dad had been a fisherman before he gave up the sea and started to work with my grandfather on the land. He was the only one in the family who showed an interest in farming. My father's family had never approved of my mother, believing that he had married below himself. No matter how hard she worked for the family, or how many of them she helped out, my father's sisters always looked down on her and took every opportunity to say something bad about us. Whenever she came back from town she would bring separate food for my grandparents, but they never seemed to be grateful and I would often find her crying over some unkind words they'd said to her. There were so many complications in the family, such as my mother's sister being married to my father's brother, and so many feuds and resentments that I didn't understand.

My aunts always believed it was important for their children to look nice. They would come asking to borrow our clothes, even though we had nothing we could really lend them. One of my older cousins was crowned 'Miss Sorsogon', beauty queen of the nearest town. She was the same age as my sister, Gang, and they were both equally pretty. Gang asked if she could go to the town to watch the crowning.

'Only if you look nice,' our aunt told her.

'I'll do my best,' Gang promised.

As the day drew closer she grew more and more excited. She dressed herself ages before she had to and was waiting eagerly to be collected.

'You look like a tramp,' our aunt scoffed when she saw her. 'I can't take you looking like that.' Gang cried for hours.

I didn't think I was that close to my eight brothers and sisters when we were kids. From what I can remember I often had arguments with Gang, Beth and Boy, all of us calling each other names, shouting at the top of our voices, furious at some tiny thing. Beth and Gang always used to boss me about, telling me to do things they should have been doing for themselves. They used to get away with it because they were older. Boy and I would fight over silly things, like a toy that Papa had made for us. We never had toys from the store; Papa made everything.

We didn't grow really close until we all had families of our own. We all care for each other so much now. Maybe we did before and just didn't realise it, and maybe part of the reason we feel so deeply for one another is because we had those happy early times together and later saw one another going through so much.

For my mother, the most recent tragedy struck short-ly before I was born. There had been a fire in the house when my older sister, Beth, went to bed with a gas light burning. She must have tipped it over in her sleep because it set light to the bundles of hemp that they made from the abaca plant to sell in the market. The abaca is a bit like the banana plant. My mother had just had a baby and the smoke and flames engulfed this newest addition to the family. Although Beth and the other children managed to get out of the house, my mother wasn't able to get the new baby out in time to save her. She tried to get her out through a window, and burned her own arms badly in the process, leaving scars that would never disappear, but it was too late. The house had a corrugated iron roof at the time, which held the heat in like a pressure cooker, and burned to the ground while my family could do little beyond watching to make sure the flames didn't spread.

The next day Dad started to build another one, using palm fronds as a thatch in the traditional manner and this replacement would be the house I would be born in. Life had to go on, even in the midst of such a terrible tragedy; there was never time to dwell on sadness.

The lost baby's name was Berhelia and she was their fourth daughter, following Sonia, Marilyn (whose nickname was Gang) and Joselyn (who was usually known as 'Beth' in the family). My father must have been desperate to have a boy to help him around the farm, but Mum just kept producing girls. By the time I came along to replace Berhelia he seemed to have given up hope because he always treated me pretty much like a boy, dressing me in shorts and t-shirts all the time. I obliged by behaving like a tomboy most of the time and he rewarded me by doing things for me like making me my own kite. Everyone made a joke of the fact that I was his favourite.

'Oh Gina,' Mum would say in despair, as she looked at my skinny little body and boy's clothes, 'how will we ever find you a husband?'

'Whatever,' I would shrug, 'I don't care.'

I wasn't sure that I wanted a husband if it meant I ended up with a stream of children and had to work as hard as my mother.

After I was born Dad's luck changed and Mum had five boys, one after the other: Raul (more usually known as Boy), Christopher, Argie, Michael and Normhel, but he continued to treat me as one of them rather than one of his girls. When Mum was carrying Normhel, Sonia (my eldest sister) was pregnant at the same time with her first – much to Mum's embarrassment. I was always closer to the older boys than I was to my sisters, stealing their clothes when mine got dirty or torn and willing to fight ferociously if they tried to get them back off me.

As soon as we were able we would all have to help with the chores: fetching water from the nearby spring to fill the drums, cleaning the house before we went to school, cooking on the charcoal fire and trudging up into the mountains to help our father with the farming. When Mum carried produce down to the town to sell on the roadsides she would take me with her and I would help in any way I could, running errands and trying to charm the customers.

One day Mum left me to look after the bananas and vegetables while she made some deliveries to our regular customers. The ticket man came to our store shouting 'Tickets ... tickets'. He wanted to be paid for the rental of our stall space, about one penny. Mum hadn't left me with any money so I told him to help himself to the bananas and eat as much as he could for payment. He seemed happy with the suggestion and helped himself to a bunch, tucking into the first one immediately. A few minutes later he left and I saw Mum coming back to the stall. I was so proud of myself I couldn't wait to tell her how I'd saved her the money with my clever business idea.

'Mama,' I said.

'Yes, *nene* (baby)?'

'I never paid the ticket man.'

'Did you tell him to come back?'

'No,' I replied, hardly able to control my proud smile. 'We won't see him again until next week.'

She asked why and I explained what I'd done.

'What?' she cried and I realised I'd made a terrible mistake.

'But Mama,' I protested. 'I saved you a penny.'

'Jesus, Gina, but what he ate was worth a lot more than one penny! Now go away, get out of my sight.'

Feeling despondent at having made such a foolish mistake, I walked aimlessly amongst the market stalls. A woman who wandered around selling fancy earrings all the time came up to me.

'Oh!' she said. 'You're so cute!'

She touched my ears and they stung a bit. Putting my fingers up to them I discovered I was wearing a pair of earrings. They were the first pair I'd ever worn and they restored my spirits immediately.

'Where is your mama?' the woman asked.

I took her over to where my mother was working, hoping she would have forgiven me for my earlier mistake and would be impressed by this woman's generosity. To my horror, the woman started asking for payment for the earrings. Mama was furious. Through my tears I tried to explain it wasn't my fault; that this woman put them into my ears without me knowing, but she obviously didn't believe me. Yet again I was costing her money.

Mum never spent money on anything except food. We had none of the ornaments that I saw in other people's houses; she bought nothing for herself.

'You can't eat ornaments,' she would scoff if I ever suggested she should treat herself to something pretty when we were in the town and had some money in our pockets at the end of a day's work.

'You can have the earrings for half price (about two pence),' the woman said when she realised Mama was going to put up a fight, but there was no way she was going to agree to that. I had to give them back and as I handed them over I felt my disappointment returning. For the rest of the day, until it was time to pack up and go home, I just kept quiet, afraid that if I made one more mistake I was going to get a smacked bottom.

They were strict parents, always quick to give us the stick if we misbehaved, and our father only had to give us one of his threatening looks for us to know we had to behave or suffer the consequences. If they had grown-up visitors around the house, Dad would just look at us and we'd know we had to stay in our bedrooms until they'd gone. We never got to talk to him about anything that might be important to us. He would never ask us about ourselves or about our lives or our dreams, he learned everything about us second-hand through Mum. That is still a big regret for me. I always wanted him to know me better and to care more about what was going on in my life and in my head.

Mum was fierce too, pushing chilli into our mouths if she ever heard us swearing and beating us with the stick if we didn't do as we were told. She didn't have any time to be patient with us, there were always too many chores waiting to be done. When she wanted to wean us off her breast milk she would rub chilli powder onto her nipples. It worked with some of us, with others it just developed a taste for spicy food which would last all our lives.

Looking back now I can see why my parents acted the way they did. But at the time I used to wonder why they felt they had to be so strict towards us. Sometimes Mama beat me for what seemed to me to be the simplest things. Afterwards I would crouch in the corner, crying, asking myself why I had to have the marks of the stick, or anything she could get her hands on at that time, all over me. Whenever I got the stick, my brothers and sisters would then tease me. No doubt they were just relieved it wasn't them being beaten, but at the time it felt as if the whole world was against me. Now I realise how difficult it must have been for Mum and Dad to control nine high-spirited children and, despite the sore bottoms we received, we all adored both our parents.

At the age of six I set off down the mountain to school in the village of Panlayaan, and that was the first time I realised my family was different to most other people's.

I already knew that villages and towns were full of strange and frightening sights from my trips to the markets with Mum. I used to hide from the policemen because they wore bright-red gloves for directing the traffic, which I thought were soaked in the blood of local people like us. I was probably right to be wary of them, even if it was for the wrong reasons. When you're so poor you have virtually no property to protect and no influence, so the police have no reason to be your friends. The first time my mother left me alone in town, while she went to buy some canisters of gas for our lights, I burst into tears, terrified the men with blood on their hands would come to get me.

On my first day at school I couldn't stop crying either. I didn't want to leave the familiar little community I'd been brought up in. I didn't want to be separated from my mother and left in a room full of strangers, all of whom seemed to be staring at me. Mum, irritated as usual by my pointless tears and eager to get on with the other business of her day, pinched me hard under the arm to shut me up.

My fears, however, proved to be well-founded and it wasn't long before the bullies smelled my vulnerability and started to pick on me. In our handed-down clothes, which we washed in the nearby river and never ironed, it was easy for the other kids to spot us as poor mountain children, scraping a living from the bottom of the barrel. They assumed we were dirty because we always had the same outfits on every day, and they knew we were poor because we only ever wore rubber flip-flops on our feet and never had any pocket money. If Mum bought me new flip-flops, which would cost just a few pennies, I would be so proud of them and so worried about losing them that I would sleep with them on. Some of the other kids actually had wristwatches and pocket money; I thought they were unbelievably lucky and assumed their families must be very rich.

'You look after those,' Mum would warn as she gave me the flip-flops, 'because if you break them you'll not be getting any more.'

Sometimes I would hunt out some guava or *santol* (a sour, orange-coloured fruit), and take them into school with me to swap for paper and pencils so that I could do my schoolwork properly. I hated to ask my parents for money because I could tell they had hardly enough as it was without these extra expenses. The other girls in the class used to gang up on me and make me hand over my fruit without giving me anything in return, and I would go home in the evenings, crying yet again, covered in bruises from their punches and kicks.

'It's no good crying to me,' Mum scolded one evening. 'Either fight them or run away from them.'

As I lay in bed that night, listening to the hum and buzz of the jungle insects outside, I pondered on her words. Although I would have liked a bit of sympathy, I could see what she meant. If I was going to go to school, which I very much wanted to do, I was going to have to accept that the bullies would always be there. I didn't intend to run away from them, my pride wouldn't allow that, so I decided to fight them instead.

The next day, when the girl who had been giving me the most trouble demanded that I hand over the guava I'd brought in with me, I refused, clutching it tightly to my chest. My heart was thumping in my ears as I commanded my feet not to turn and run. When she started hitting me my anger overcame my fear and I flew at her, dropping the guava. I landed on her back, sticking like a leech, pulling her hair and sinking my teeth into the top of her head. The others drew back and watched in amazement. No one tried to snatch the fallen guava. That night my tormentor was the one who went home crying and her mother came to see Mum to complain about my wild behaviour.

'I told you not to be naughty!' Mum said once the woman had gone, shocked by my sudden change in character.

'You told me to fight back!' I protested, but I got the stick anyway, for causing her trouble again and bringing shame on the family.

'You were always the naughtiest of my children,' Mum told me years later. 'But you were the most caring as well. You were always hiding from me, making me run around looking for you.'

I can remember that; going to my grandmother's house for sanctuary or hiding for hours under one of the beds, listening to Mum shouting my name.

The house was very sparsely furnished. Dad was a carpenter as well as a farmer and he made us beds and a settee from the lumber on our land, which saved the family a lot of money. We wouldn't have been able to buy furniture from shops. If he hadn't built the beds we would have been sleeping on the floor.

The school was a kilometre away from the house, which took a long time to walk when our legs were still little. Raul and I would set off home for lunch and by the time we got there it was time to be back in school. By the time we got back to the classroom it was time to come home again. Most of our days were spent walking back and forth through dust or puddles, depending on the weather, clutching our few books and talking non-stop.

Because we had nothing to carry our schoolwork in, we used to compete ferociously for any plastic bags that my father might bring home with him at the end of a working day. We would watch for his approach and if we saw he was carrying something in a bag we would race each other to get to him first to beg to be given it. If Raul won the race I would become furious, hitting him until he either gave up the prized bag or managed to escape me.

The rule in the family was that whenever we weren't at school we all had to climb the five kilometres to our land in the mountains with our father, to help him work, carrying bananas, yams, lumber or whatever else we could manage back down to the house for our mother to cook or take to market. It was hard, painful work and I sometimes used to pray to be ill so I would be allowed to stay at home and have Mum take care of me. If I was ill I might even get a biscuit or a sweet while everyone else was out, treats that would normally be forbidden. At the same time, I wanted to find a way to lighten my parents' workload.

'If we don't work,' Dad would say whenever we complained we were too tired, 'we don't eat.'

Sometimes I used to stand, staring up at the clouds in the sky, trying to imagine what my life would be like when I grew up and how I might be able to make my parents' lives easier. I used to pray for help from God. My parents were very religious, especially my mother. We would go to the Catholic church at San Vincente every week and in the house Mum had a battered little statue of an angel which she would kneel down in front of each night.

'Children,' she would say, 'kneel behind me.'

I was happy to obey, eager to please a God who might help me to make life easier for myself and my family.

Despite all the difficulties, both my parents were keen on us getting as much education as possible.

'You don't want to end up going to work in the mountains the whole of your lives like we do,' Dad would tell us. 'You need education so you can get proper jobs and travel abroad.'

I had no idea what other sorts of jobs they thought they were educating us for, or where they thought we would travel, and I doubt if they did either, but Dad would become very cross if I brought home a bad report card. So anxious was I to avoid his wrath that I would only show him the good ones, forging his signature on the others and telling him we hadn't been given them that week.

People were always talking about going abroad to work and it was considered a great status symbol for a family to have someone sending home money. I would eavesdrop on their stories whenever they came back for visits with wonder and bewilderment. Manila sounded as foreign and strange to me as America, England or Dubai. I couldn't imagine for a second what these places might be like. Since there was no television in our province I didn't get to see any films of these exotic sounding locations either. The only pictures were the ones that grew in my imagination. A small part of me wanted to go to all these places and have adventures of my own to talk about, but most of me was terrified at the thought of going anywhere.

Any money my mother did manage to save she would lock in a cupboard, ready for emergencies. People like my parents had no one to turn to if one of us became ill or suffered a catastrophe like a fire; they only had what they could scrape together each day. She kept the key to the cupboard on a string around her waist at all times, even when she was bathing. Even though the cupboard was later swept away in a typhoon, she still keeps the key round her waist to this day, along with others.

Mum always taught us we must be honest and never steal. One day she brought home a basket of tuna fish from the town, as she often did, enough to last us for the whole week. There was a particular dish she often made in a big saucepan, calling it 'tomato sardines' and rationing it out over the days. It always tasted beautiful. That day Raul and I had gone without our breakfast as a punishment for not cleaning the house before going to school. By the time we got home in the afternoon, having had nothing to eat all day, we were truly starving. There was no one in the house when we got there and I noticed the saucepan hanging in the roof space, out of reach of the dogs, cats and rats.

'Bring it down,' I told my brother, who was already taller than me.

'No,' he said, too frightened of what our mother would say if she caught us.

'Go on,' I coaxed, 'aren't you hungry? It's tomato sardines.'

I could see from his eyes he was as tempted as I was and eventually he gave in to my cajoling. Once we'd lifted the lid and smelt the fish, there was no way we could resist and we had practically cleaned the pan before I told him to put it back.

'Time for tea,' Mum said when she came home a few hours later, and my heart sank like a stone, remembering what had happened to the cat who had stolen her fish before. 'Get the saucepan down, Gina.'

'You do it, Beth,' I told my sister and walked towards the door.

'Where are you going?' Mum asked, puzzled as to why I would leave just as she was about to serve up my favourite dish.

'I'm not hungry,' I said.

'Me neither,' said my brother, hurrying to catch me up.

'Gina! Boy!' she shouted as we hurried away. 'Have you eaten the fish?'

There was no hope of denying it and we both had very sore bottoms when we went to bed that night. For the next week we were given nothing but plain rice. Never again was I tempted to take more than my fair share from the family pot. We knew we'd done wrong because we had always been taught how important it was not to be greedy and to share the food equally, even when it was just rice, but that fish had been so delicious and our stomachs had been so empty we had given in to temptation.

When I was about nine years old, Sonia (my eldest sister) was at college, studying to become a fashion designer, and Mum and Dad had arranged for her to marry a boy they approved of. Unfortunately, Sonia hadn't agreed with their choice and had started courting another boy called Leonardo.

One of my dad's sisters-in-law saw them together and, eager to cause trouble, made it her business to inform him about what was going on behind his back.

'Every time Sonia goes to school she's seeing some-one else,' she said, pretending she was speaking out of concern for her niece's well-being.

It was only a couple of months before Sonia would finish her course, but Dad was so furious at finding out about Leonardo in this way he stopped her going to school. He was determined to keep them apart.

Soon after this, Mum and Dad had a big argument, which started over something silly. Dad wanted a cup of coffee and he found that Mum, who made herself coffee all day long, had used the last of the sugar. We all drank a lot of coffee, picking the beans from our own trees, drying them in the sun and breaking the husks off with wooden pestles and mortars fashioned from our own lumber. We would then fry the coffee until it was black, and strain it through a fine sieve, drinking it strong, with sugar but no milk.

I don't think the sugar itself was actually that impor-tant; it was just the final straw for him in a life filled with difficulties and frustrations. Dad had been ill for a while and Mum had been nagging him and accusing him of being lazy. The tension had been building and the sugar was the spark that lit the powder keg. The row grew out of all proportion as they heaped more and more grievances onto the flames and there was nothing we children could do apart from listen in horror as they shouted and threatened one another, letting out all the anger that must have been building up inside them for years. It ended with my father storming out of the house with a bag, announcing he was going to Manila.

We didn't really understand what was going on, all we knew was that Dad was gone and Mum was crying all the time, but it wasn't that unusual for grown-ups to just disappear from our lives for a few months at a time in order to earn some money. None of the adults wanted to talk to us about it. Manila was a strange and distant-sounding place to us, somewhere from another world.

His departure seemed to release all sorts of bad feelings and some of Dad's relatives took advantage of his absence to bully and taunt us, saying we would never see him again. Maybe they were pleased he had finally left Mum and wanted to widen the rift in the hope that she would give up on the marriage.

We didn't have much time to think about how sad we felt, because we had to keep things going on the farm without him. Every day we would trudge into the mountains, sometimes twice a day, to do the jobs that he would have done. Mum never complained about the extra work or the abuse she received from her in-laws, even lending some of her precious savings to Dad's sisters when they needed help.

But I often saw her crying when she didn't think anyone was around, especially when Dad's sisters gleefully told her he had another woman in Manila. When they showed her a photograph of the woman, she was beside herself with fury, deciding she was going to end the marriage and that we all had to choose whether we stayed with her or went to live with him.

'Who wants to go with me?' she asked us all and everyone except me put their hands up. 'Right,' she said, 'Gina can go with her beloved father, then!'

'I don't want to go with either of you,' I replied. 'I don't want to choose between you. I don't want to hurt either of you. I'd rather go and live with Nana.'

The row calmed down as we went back to our routine of daily drudgery without him and Mum didn't talk about divorce any more, just concentrating on surviving. My heart was heavy at the thought that Dad might have found someone he preferred to us. One day, when we were working in the mountains, I looked up at the sky and prayed to the Lord to bring my parents back together.

'Lord, let me have all the pain instead of Mama,' I begged.

I wanted to be able to make their life easier. I loved them both so much I didn't want them to be apart. Manila was a 12-hour bus ride away and it seemed like the end of the world. I felt so helpless.

The aunt who had told on Sonia always enjoyed stirring up trouble in Dad's family, maybe because she was jealous of us for some reason. Her mischief-making with Sonia had proved very successful, and when my father departed for Manila with his bag, Mum was left to deal with the broken-hearted Sonia on her own.

One morning, when Mum was away in Sorsogon selling bananas, Sonia woke me up. She had a shirt tied
around her head, which looked strange, and she gave me
a small bag of something, telling me to throw it away. I
had no idea what it was at first but I was frightened
when I saw there was blood on her hands.

'Shhh,' she ordered me. 'Don't say anything to Boy or
the others, they mustn't know.'

It turned out that in a fit of anger she'd cut off all her
hair with galvanised scissors, gouging chunks out of her
scalp in the process. When Mum got home I was so
frightened I blurted out everything and she didn't seem
to know whether to laugh or cry.

The tradition in the Philippines is for a young man to
visit the parents of the girl he is courting and to offer his
assistance in any way possible. Leonardo was so in love he
was not going to give up that easily and he was more
than happy to come and help the family every day since
he didn't live far away. But Sonia was terrified of him
seeing her now that she had made such a mess of her
head.

'You'll have to hide under the bed whenever he
comes to the house,' Mum told her. 'We'll tell him you've
gone to Manila.'

In a small community like ours, however, we couldn't
risk anyone else seeing her either, in case they told
Leonardo, so for the next three months Sonia spent most
of her time under the bed waiting for her hair to grow,

sometimes not even able to come out for meals because my cousins would be playing around the house with me. We didn't even tell the boys she was there. As far as everyone was concerned she was in Manila. Our relatives must have suspected something was up because they used to creep up to the house and try to peer through the shutters to catch us out.

Leonardo, however, was not put off by such a temporary setback and continued to come calling with offers of assistance.

'You have to stop coming,' Mum would screech at him. 'People will think you're courting me and Sonia both, with her and her father away.'

'It's all right, Mama,' he would smile innocently. 'I just want to help.'

He was such a kind boy, often bringing me sweets and obviously so in love with my sister, that I took pity on him. There had never been any way I could resist a bag of sweets.

'Where has Sonia gone?' he asked me one day, after giving me the bag he'd brought with him.

'You mustn't tell anyone,' I whispered as I chewed, 'but she's hiding under the bed. You must just wait for her to come out. Don't tell anyone I told you or they'll kill me.'

He was such a nice man he never said a word. He kept on coming to visit and doing chores until Sonia felt able to emerge back into the light, as if she had just got off the bus from Manila.

The other problem was that Dad had heard from his relatives that his eldest daughter was somewhere in the same city as him. He kept writing and sending messages asking where Sonia was staying so he could visit her, and Mum kept having to find excuses not to tell him.

A year later my prayers were answered and Dad came back home, raising me high in the air when I ran out to greet him. Everything we'd been told had been lies; he'd actually stayed in Manila, working as a labourer in a bottling factory, in order to make enough money to try to lift the family off the poverty line. While the mountains could supply us with enough food to survive, we needed something else to make a bit of extra money if we were ever to have any real security. He now had the capital he needed to start a little coffee shop and grocery store in the town of Bintan-o, and to build another wooden house in the same village. This house would be smaller and even simpler than the mountain house, but it would give us a chance to mix with other people.

'Now you children are getting older,' Dad told us, 'you need to spend more time in the town.'

It meant that as a family we now had twice as much work to do, since we still had to go back to take care of the farm, but at least we were able to earn a bit more money and we were no longer isolated from the rest of the world. There were some stone-built houses in the village, belonging to families who seemed enormously rich to us because they had smart clean clothes and proper shoes. Some of them even had shiny motorbikes and cars, not having to travel everywhere in the crowded local buses or the brightly decorated jeepneys which local people had customised from old US army jeeps and used as shared local taxis.

I didn't care where we were or what we were doing for a living, just as long as my mum and dad were together again. I so much wanted to find a way to make their lives easier. My brother and I would live in the mountain house during the week, so we could get to school easily, only going to Bintan-o during weekends and holidays. Dad would come to the farm most days, taking fruit and vegetables back to sell in the shop.

Although I spent most of my time dreaming of being a teacher, I loved to sing and dance as well, particularly for my teachers at school. I used to dance to 'Don't Cry for me Argentina' and 'Time After Time', as well as to the local music that Mum would play on her old battery-driven record player. I used to love to dress up in my sisters' clothes and shoes and perform for her in the evenings.

'When I'm grown up I want to be a dancer,' I would tell her.

'Don't be dreaming too much, Gina,' Mum warned.

'I know Mum,' I assured her, 'I'm only joking. I want to be a teacher really.'

We could never have new clothes because if Mum bought something for one of us the rest of us would become jealous. But then two of my cousins came to live with us. Their mother was Mum's sister and they were quite a bit older than me. It seemed that they could have new clothes whenever they wanted, even though we couldn't, and the unfairness of it made me cry.

I must have made my dislike of them very obvious because one of them started telling Mum stories about things I'd done or not done. I got blamed for every little thing that happened. Eventually, I lost my temper and suggested that since they were grown-ups they should get jobs and contribute towards the family budget.

Mum went mad at me for being so disrespectful and took the stick to me. I hadn't meant to be disrespectful, I just wanted to help my parents by taking away some of the burdens that weighed them down and I didn't see why these women couldn't help instead of adding to the problem. I realised there was nothing I could do to make them change their ways, that if I wanted to help my parents I was going to have to do it myself.

I was nearly eleven at the time and due to move up to the High School. I'd been looking forward to it and had been trying on my older sister's uniform in preparation. But I decided it wouldn't be fair of me to go on at school when my parents had so many mouths to feed. I decided I must start to pull my weight, like my older sisters.

'I'm going to Manila,' I announced, as if I did such things every day, 'to get a job and earn some money.'

CHAPTER TWO

In Service in the City

A lady I didn't know had been talking to Mum in the village. Mum must have told her about my plan to go to Manila to look for work, probably saying how worried she was about her 11-year-old daughter going on such a long journey on her own to a big, strange city.

'I'm going back to Manila too,' the woman told her, 'and I know of a family who are looking for a maid. Why don't I take Gina with me and drop her off at their house?'

Mum must have thought that was a better idea than me going to the city on my own and then walking the streets looking for a job, even though she had no idea who this family was or whether they would be kind to me. So many girls in the Philippines go to be maids in other people's houses, sometimes travelling across whole continents in search of employment. Everyone is used to the risks involved and knows they're inevitable, but that doesn't mean a parent doesn't worry. She'd tried her hardest to dissuade me from my plan, telling me stories of other girls she'd heard about who had ended up being virtual slaves to their employers, working 24 hours a day for no money. She hinted at darker things too and I knew that some of the girls had come back home pregnant with unwanted babies. Even as she was telling me these things I think she knew that once I'd made up my mind nothing would change it. Perhaps I reminded her of herself at my age.

The bus was hot and crowded as we boarded it in the late afternoon a few days later, and it became more so in the course of the 12-hour drive as we took on more and more passengers along the way, many of them struggling under the weight of their own luggage. At least when we were moving there was a draft from the open windows, even if it did sometimes bring in more dust than air.

We would stop every few hours at garages where we could buy drinks and use the toilets, and in between I watched the night-time scenery speeding past, gradually changing from moonlit mountains and small settlements nestling in the jungle, to better lit streets and sturdier houses as we came into the outskirts of the great sprawling city. I dozed fitfully, too nervous about what lay ahead to really relax, too tired to be able to keep my eyes open all the time.

There were so many different stops in Manila, every street looking the same to me. I don't know how I would ever have found the right one without the help of my travelling companion. She pointed out the house to me as we drew up and waved cheerfully from the window of the bus as it pulled away, having deposited me and my plastic bag of belongings on the sidewalk.

I paused for a second to take in my surroundings and gather my thoughts. It looked like a rich area to me. There were rows of neatly built stone houses, many with shiny family cars parked outside, glinting in the early morning sun, waiting for their owners to drive them to work. Everything was orderly and everything had its place, except me.

When the bus has finally vanished from sight and the rumble of its engine had faded away, I took a deep breath, mustering all my courage, and walked up the path, past neatly clipped lawns to the front door. I rang the bell, hoping I wouldn't be waking anyone up.

'Hello,' I said shyly when a lady opened the door. 'I heard you were looking for a maid. I've been recommended by ... someone.'

I gestured vaguely at the road where the bus had been a few moments before, realising I had no idea what the lady's name was.

The woman was obviously startled by my unannounced arrival and called her husband, inviting me into the house to sit down. Her husband appeared from upstairs, looking as if he had just showered and got dressed in preparation for the day. They seemed to be shocked by how tiny I was and unsure what to do with me now I was sitting in their house.

'So, you want to be a maid?' the woman asked, making sure she understood what was going on.

'Yes, please,' I replied, as politely as I knew how.

'But you're only a kid,' the husband said.

'I may be,' I agreed, 'but I'll try my best and work hard. I'm used to helping my mother at home.'

My overwhelming feeling at that moment was tiredness, having been awake for most of the journey and the whole day before that during the preparations for the trip. The excitement had been building inside me for days and, now I was here, I felt an urgent need to lie down and close my eyes. They must have been able to see how heavy my lids were and how hard I was struggling to keep them open. Apparently resigning themselves to the fact that I'd become their responsibility, whether they liked it or not, they showed me to the bedroom I would be sharing with their daughters and I fell almost instantly into a deep, dream-filled sleep.

Just before I sank into oblivion I heard the couple talking outside the room.

'But she's just a child,' the husband was saying.

'We can at least give her a chance,' his wife suggested. 'We can hardly send her all the way back. Maybe she'll be a fast learner. I do need some help around the house.'

I slept all through the first day and when I woke up I was worried they would think I was lazy and sack me before I'd even started. But the lady of the house seemed very happy to see me when I emerged, blinking nervously, from the bedroom, and she showed me what she would want me to do if I was going to stay. I would have cleaning and washing duties around the house, but she also wanted me to cook for the family as well. I'd helped my mother and sisters a little with the preparation of food at home, but always the simplest dishes. Now I had to learn how to clean and cook fish properly and provide really nice meals. Once the meals were ready I could then sit down with them to eat.

My employers owned a fish business, which obviously kept them comfortably off, although they had no other servants apart from me. They had two sons and two daughters, all older than me and all pleased to welcome me into their home.

I worked as hard as I could, learning the necessary skills quickly, eager to please them, and they were very kind to me in return, treating me almost like one of the family. At the same time I was excited to be in the big city, even though I never ventured far from the streets around the house. I was frightened that if I strayed too far I would become lost in the maze of back streets and I would never be able to find my way back home. I'd seen from the bus how many of the different areas looked the same. With my wages I bought myself some nice clothes for the first time, and sent money home to Mum. I felt so grown up and proud of myself as I put the envelope in the post. Not only had I made it easier for them by giving them one less mouth to feed, I was even contributing to Mum's savings.

My bosses' eldest son, who must have been about 25 years old, was always very friendly. One day I could hear him calling to me from the bathroom.

'Gina!'

'Yes, *Kuya*,' I replied, using the respectful term for 'big brother'.

'Pass me a flannel, will you?'

'Yes, *Kuya*,' I said.

When I went into the bathroom he was standing in the shower, completely naked. It should have been obvious to me where he would be because I'd heard the sound of running water from outside, but I was still so young and innocent and the unexpected sight of a naked man shocked me so much it made me shake physically.

'Don't tell my mum and dad that you've seen me like this,' he said, suddenly nervous when he saw my reaction and unsure what to do next.

I stayed silent, unable to find the correct words for such a situation. Eventually deciding to go on about my business as if nothing unusual had happened, I left the room as quickly as possible and never mentioned the incident again to anyone. The feelings of fear and vulnerability that the shock had sown in me kept me awake at night, making me feel unsafe and far from home. I lay in my bed and cried silently for my mother and my brothers and sisters, covering my face with the sheet so that the girls wouldn't hear me and ask what was wrong. During the days I continued to be very happy because of the way they all treated me, as if I was no different to them, but each night the sadness returned.

One night a few weeks later everyone was going out except for the older brother and I realised as I went to my bedroom that he and I were going to be alone in the house for several hours. I closed the bedroom door firmly, wishing there was a lock on the inside, and climbed into the bed with my shorts and t-shirt on, pulling the sheets tightly around me as protection against my fears. I had no idea what might happen; I just knew I was frightened. I wanted to get to sleep as quickly as possible and wake up to find everyone back in the house and life going on as normal.

I heard him coming into the room a little while later, but I kept my eyes tight shut, hoping that if he thought I was asleep he would just go back to his own room. I could sense the heat from his body as he came closer to my bed and I tightened every muscle to stop myself from shaking and giving myself away. When I felt his hand touching the sheet I couldn't stop myself from crying out in shock.

'Don't worry, don't worry,' he said, backing away. 'Don't tell my mother that I came in here.'

I watched as he retreated from the room, closing the door behind him. I had no idea what he'd been planning or hoping for, or whether he would be back. I just knew I wanted to go home.

I never said anything to my boss about what had happened, but from that moment on my homesickness grew stronger every day. Even though my bosses' daughters treated me like a sister, I wanted to see my own brothers and sisters again. I wanted to go back to my childhood home, recapture that feeling of security and stop pretending to be a grown-up for a little bit longer.

'I want to go home,' I told my boss eventually.

'Oh.' She looked so sad, I felt guilty. 'But we like you so much. Please stay with us. You're probably just a little homesick and the feeling will pass.'

Her husband said the same when he came home. 'What can we do to make you stay?' he asked.

'Would you like me to make you a new set of clothes?' his wife, who was also a seamstress, asked.

'My grandma just died,' I lied, immediately feeling even more guilty about deceiving them, but unable to think of any other excuse. 'So my family want me to go home.'

They kept trying to dissuade me but I just kept crying, and eventually they relented and said it was up to me. I could tell they were angry with me because the atmosphere in the house had changed. I didn't want to be there any more but I didn't yet have enough money for the bus fare home. I went next door to the neighbouring family, who I'd become friendly with during my time in the house.

'Please can I stay with you?' I asked.

'Of course you can,' they said, immediately able to see that I was in a bad state.

'I want to go home,' I told them.

To earn the money for the bus fare I helped my new family around the house for a few weeks and they bought my ticket for me. My former employers must have been hurt that I'd walked out on them like that, but I was too young and too inexperienced to know what to do to make things better with them. I would never have dared to tell them that their son's behaviour was one of the main reasons I wanted to go home.

Once I was on the bus and it was drawing away from the stop, I felt the excitement tightening inside me at the thought of seeing my family again after such a long time. I'd been dreaming of this moment for so many weeks, half afraid that it would never come. I could hardly wait for the journey to be over as the bus ground its way out of the city towards the mountains I was longing to see again.

CHAPTER THREE

Working for Auntie

When the bus deposited me back in my hometown I felt like I had returned as a completely different person to the little girl who had left a few months before. Now that I could puff out my chest and say 'I've been to Manila', I believed I could sound like the grown-ups, like all the girls who came back, casually dropping the exotic names of the cities and countries they'd travelled to and worked in like badges of honour. No one at home needed to know how homesick I'd been, or how frightened when a man had come into my bedroom. All they needed to know was that the little tomboy, Gina, had 'been to Manila' and earned her own keep.

Everyone seemed pleased to see me, eager to tell me all the gossip from home even though I was too exhausted from the journey to be able to take it in. No one bothered to ask me any questions about where I'd been and what I might have experienced, they just wanted to make a fuss of me. It was exciting to be the centre of attention and I must have grown up a little physically in those months I was away because I noticed a few of the local boys were treating me differently, edging towards courting me, even though I was still only 12 and looked young for my age. I might have started developing in other ways, but I hadn't grown much taller. Back on home territory, with my family around to protect me, I felt safe enough to flirt and lead the boys on a little, as if I'd suddenly become a woman of the world.

People kept telling me I'd become beautiful. Maybe they'd just taken me for granted before and now they were seeing me through new eyes, or maybe it was because I'd come back wearing pretty girls' clothes from the city, not shorts and shirts from the second-hand shop like my brothers. Whatever the reason, I liked to hear the compliments, even if I didn't know how to respond beyond blushing and giggling or pretending I hadn't heard.

'So,' Mum said, when the excitement of my homecoming had settled down and it was just the two of us. 'Are you going to go back to school now?'

'No,' I shook my head.

I'd given the matter a lot of thought on the journey home, as I stared out the window at the passing scenery for hours on end, and the thought of returning to the classroom and the daily battles with the bullies was too much to contemplate. I was embarrassed at the thought of rejoining the class after missing so many months of study, knowing that the younger kids would have moved ahead in my absence and would mock my ignorance even more. There seemed no point in going back now; it was too late to hope that I would catch up enough to become a teacher. That now seemed like no more than the foolish dreams of a child.

I'd become used to being treated like a grown-up and having a little money of my own from time to time. The idea of once again being just another mouth for my parents to feed was unthinkable. I wanted to support myself and contribute to the family. At the same time I didn't want to go away and live with strangers again, not yet anyway.

'I think I'll ask Auntie if I can work for her,' I said.

My auntie lived in the town of Sorsogon, where she ran a successful dry goods shop and employed a number of people. Rather than a 12-hour bus ride, Sorsogon was just a short ride in the side car of a 'tricycle', which was what we called the motorbike taxis that drove their customers from village to village, swerving round the bumps and puddles and the occasional grazing carabaw. She was a relative of my Dad's and needed someone to do the washing, cleaning and cooking for all the people who lived in her house and worked in her shop. Mum didn't much like the idea of me going to work for a part of the family which held her in such contempt, but she could see my mind was made up and after a few attempts to sell me on the idea of going back to school she gave up. I took the ride into town and knocked on Auntie's door to offer my services.

Auntie always looked old to me, even though she was probably only middle-aged, and never seemed to smile. It was as if she believed everything that happened around her was part of a plot to steal her money and make her life more difficult than it already was. In fact her life was extremely easy as far as I could see.

I knew she looked down on my mother and the rest of my family, believing that she was something better, but she was the only family member I knew who would be in a position to offer me a wage. In a way I suppose that did give her an advantage over the rest of us. She wasn't rich but she knew how to make money and, more importantly, she knew how to hang on to it.

'You can do the cooking and cleaning,' she said once she'd interrogated me thoroughly. She agreed to pay me the equivalent of one pound a month, but I had to understand that any breakages would be deducted from my pay.

I didn't care that the money was less than I'd been earning in Manila and that she seemed to think I was part of some lower species. At least I wouldn't be costing my family anything and I might even be able to save some of my wages to give to my mother since there wasn't much to spend your money on in Sorsogon. Just to be earning at all made me feel proud and I knew that at my age I wouldn't be able to earn any more in a small town like that.

Because I wanted to work there I agreed to the terms without even asking how many people I would be cooking for each day. I soon discovered there were 15 of us in all and I was responsible for feeding everyone. I slept in a big room filled with bunk beds where everyone who worked for my auntie stayed. She and her immediate family had their own separate rooms. There was another helper employed to do the washing for everyone living in the house. Many of them were physically big people who wore large or extra-large sizes. Their clothes would get filthy in the shop and everything had to be scrubbed by hand in the sink every day and hung out to dry in the sun before coming in to be ironed. There was never a moment in the day when there weren't chores to be done.

We would both get up at six in the morning and would be working solidly until it was time to go to bed again, our only breaks were meal times, during which I still had to serve everyone and clear up afterwards. I would start each day by cleaning the house, which had four bedrooms and two toilets. I was only allowed to clean Auntie's room if she was there because she didn't trust me not to steal something. I suppose she thought that because I came from the poorer side of the family I was automatically a thief and couldn't be trusted.

By eight o'clock I would be out doing the day's shopping before the sun had become too hot, buying the necessary vegetables, fish and meat. Once I got it back home I would have to clean everything up, prepare and cook the first meal of the day. Auntie kept a firm watch on my spending. I wasn't allowed to buy minced meat, for instance, I had to buy it whole and mince it myself at home, using an old manual machine with a handle that took all my strength to turn. One day, when I was running out of time, I tried to rush the process. The meat became stuck in the mincer and I forced it, leaning all my weight on the handle, breaking the machine.

'You'll have to pay for that you clumsy girl!' Auntie shouted when she found out, and it took me nearly two years to finish paying that debt.

Once I'd prepared the food I then had to carry it across to the store for the staff who had been working there since dawn.

Sometimes Auntie's husband, who was a Chinese man, would take pity on me and do something nice like buy me a Coke.

'Why did you ask your uncle to buy you a Coke?' Auntie would shout when she found out that he'd been squandering her money.

'I didn't ask him,' I would protest, 'he gave it to me.'

But she would refuse to believe me. In her eyes I was a scrounger and a parasite who would try to get away with whatever I could. She had no intention of allowing such a thing to happen.

She was always determined to think the worst of me. If I ever asked to go home to visit my mother she'd order me to strip in front of her and would search through my clothes and carrier bags to make sure I wasn't trying to steal anything from her, like some of her daughter's underwear. I did used to get quite jealous of my cousin because she seemed to have hundreds of pairs of jeans, many of which she never wore, and I thought she might at least have offered to give me one pair, seeing how I was struggling to manage on my wages. By that time I'd put on a little puppy fat and I was chubby enough to have fitted anything she gave me. Sometimes she used to show me her cupboards, apparently unaware of the fact that I had nothing of my own.

'Oh, Gina,' she'd sigh, 'I don't know what to do with all my clothes.'

In her eyes, like those of her mother, I was just the maid and so they paid no thought to what I might need, or to my feelings, and my pride wouldn't allow me to speak out.

When Auntie's son became engaged to a very pretty girl who had been a helper to one of his sisters, the girl moved into the house as well. When her relatives started to arrive from Manila on visits I had to cook for them too. The fiancée was a sweet girl who would often talk to me as an equal, no doubt remembering how it felt to be treated as a servant, but if Auntie caught us I would be scolded for not getting on with my work. She always made it obvious she saw me as something less than the other people in her family, and I was hurt.

Later, when I needed a change of routine, I swapped my jobs in the house from cleaning and cooking to washing and ironing. Whenever I was ironing my cousin's clothes they seemed such good quality to me. I hoped I would be able to afford something as luxurious when I was older, both for myself and for my parents and brothers and sisters.

Despite Auntie's tirades, her husband continued trying to be helpful and kind to all the staff, buying us soap and shampoo and toothpaste, so we didn't have to use up our wages on daily necessities. Auntie was constantly getting on at him for wasting her money on such things.

'You shouldn't let them talk you into giving them so much,' she'd tell him. 'They earn wages, they should buy their own supplies.'

Every year typhoons attack the Philippines, leaving devastation in their wake. That year, 1987, as I lay in my auntie's solid stone house, listening to the roar of the wind outside, I thought of my family in their little wooden home, remembering back to other years when we huddled together nervously listening to the howling gales and crashing rains, wondering whether or not the roof and walls would be ripped away from around us. Listening to extremes of weather still makes me feel small and vulnerable. The forces of nature are always visible in lands like the Philippines, as the whole world realised on Boxing Day in 2004, when a giant tsunami swept across the region killing hundreds of thousands of people, including many Western tourists enjoying beach holidays in places like Phuket and Sri Lanka.

I finally managed to get to sleep that night in 1987 despite the roar of the winds. By the time we woke up the following morning they'd died down and the sun was shining as if nothing had ever happened, making the puddles and wet jungle leaves steam peacefully. But the wreckage in the streets bore witness to how ferocious the storms had been. The following week was my 14th birthday and I was planning to go home to Bintan-o to celebrate with my family. I guessed there would still be lots of clearing up for me to help with when I got there since the village was right by the sea. Everyone was talking about how bad the winds had been and there were reports coming in of giant waves hitting villages on the coast. I began to worry. The typhoon had been christened Sisang.

Later that morning, as I worked in the kitchen, I heard a commotion at the door and I went to see what was happening. It was a few seconds before I realised that the bedraggled bunch of people standing outside, their drenched clothes hanging off them in tatters, were my family. Many of them had cuts on their heads and limbs and the blood was still wet as it mingled with the dirt and water.

'What happened?' I wanted to know, but everyone was talking and shouting at once and it was hard to work out what they were telling us.

Slowly the picture emerged from the chaos; the typhoon had whipped up a giant wave out at sea and it had swept in over the beaches and through Bintan-o, taking many buildings, including our family home, with it.

'The house is damaged?' I asked.

'It's gone,' Mum said, crying as she talked. 'Everything has been blown away. There's nothing left.'

'We had no control,' one of my brothers told me, 'we just had to go where the wave took us, carried away like pieces of driftwood.'

'There were dead bodies everywhere,' Dad said. 'We were walking through them, looking for family members.'

Auntie wouldn't allow them into her nice clean house in such a terrible state, so I cuddled them where they stood in the street, crying with them for everything they'd lost. They seemed small and helpless in the face of such a catastrophe. My father had worked so hard to build that house and the business, and it had all been washed away in just a few hours. We knew nothing about things like insurance. There would be no compensation or help from anywhere. They were going to have pick themselves up and start all over again, as always.

When they realised Auntie wasn't going to invite them into the house, not even to wash or clean up their wounds or have a bite to eat, they prepared themselves to leave.

'Where are you going to go?' I asked.

'We'll go back to the house in the mountains and see what the damage has been up there,' Mum said. 'Maybe it won't be so bad.'

As I stood, watching them walk away, their heads down and their feet dragging with exhaustion, I felt the strongest urge to run after them, to be with them at this terrible time and to help them. But I knew it was more important I tried to persuade Auntie to lend me some money and I wouldn't be able to do that if I deserted my job without giving her time to find a replacement. Then, when I went to visit them, I would be able to give them something practical and useful. I wanted so much to help them and I vowed that as soon as I could find a way to make money I would build them a stone house with solid foundations, so they could sleep safely in their beds and would never have to fear the weather again.

When they got back to the farm they found the wind and driving rains had destroyed all the crops. They could salvage almost nothing from amongst the mudslides and fallen trees which made the journey up twice as arduous as before, blocking paths and washing away steps.

I know now that international agencies and charities sent aid to the Philippines after Sisang struck, but we knew nothing about it at the time. Whoever benefited from the money and supplies sent, it wasn't people like my family. We eventually discovered that Sisang had killed 650 people in the region that night and left half a million homeless. My family were lucky to be alive and to have another roof to shelter under.

'Auntie,' I said, later that day, when my tears had calmed enough to allow me to speak, 'please can I borrow some money to help my family?'

'Borrow money?' she looked at me incredulously. 'How will you ever pay it back?'

'I'll work for no wages until the debt is paid,' I promised. 'I have to be able to do something for them.'

Eventually she gave in to my pleading and tears and lent me the equivalent of £10.

'Just make sure you stay here until it's all paid back,' she said as she reluctantly handed it over.

It took me more than a year to work that debt off. Not only did she charge me for any broken glasses and plates, I also had to pay for anything I damaged when ironing. When Auntie's daughter asked me to iron her husband's security guard uniform, I made a mistake with the iron, which was heated on charcoal and impossible to adjust, and burnt the jacket.

'I'm so sorry,' I said, unable to stop the tears brimming to my eyes, knowing I was going to be in trouble.

'You will be sorry,' Auntie said, 'because I'm going to charge you for it.'

That was another three months' money gone. How was I ever going to be able to raise enough to help my family build a stone house at this rate?

CHAPTER FOUR

Marriage and Motherhood

I'd been at Auntie's for four years when I first spotted Jun working across the road from the house. I was 15. For all that time I'd spent virtually every day shopping, cooking, cleaning, washing or ironing for other people, with no time for myself or to make any friends outside the family or the workers in the house and the shop. I didn't mind that because I'd never known any different.

In the many hours I had to daydream, while doing the same repetitive tasks day in and day out, I'd been beginning to think about going back to Manila now that I was older and felt more confident about looking after myself. Half planning and half dreaming, I was trying to see a way of breaking the cycle of poverty that had been surrounding my family for so many years. I could see I was never going to make any money for my mum and dad if I stayed at my auntie's, and there weren't many opportunities to do anything better in Sorsogon.

When my thoughts wandered back to my first stay in Manila, I felt a twinge of nostalgia for the excitement of arriving in the big, strange city with the feeling that anything could happen. I remembered the buzz of adrenaline I experienced when I first stepped off the bus into an alien world and I felt I was ready for another big adventure. It wasn't that easy, however, to do anything with my life when I had no money and every month my aunt found another excuse to dock my wages. I needed a job to go to or a sponsor to buy me a ticket and help me get a foot on the ladder. My mum had paid for my ticket the first time I travelled to Manila, but I couldn't ask her to do that again, not after everything that had happened.

Then Jun came along and all my dreams changed course. He worked in the warehouse of a local department store and would often be sitting or standing around outside the storeroom doors with his friends and workmates, smoking, laughing and talking, taking the air and watching the world go by. The first time I saw him it felt as if I'd had an electric shock; just a glimpse of his face made my heart beat faster and the blood rush to my cheeks. I was even having trouble breathing. I'd never experienced such a feeling before and for a second I was alarmed, wondering if perhaps I was being taken ill.

Over the following days I found myself thinking all the time about that feeling and about the boy who had induced it, wanting to do something about it but not knowing what that might be. Life suddenly seemed full of possibilities and promise, but at the same time there was the frightening thought that it might all come to nothing if I didn't do something about it. But what could a girl like me do about anything like that without seeming forward and inappropriate? It was all an agonising and tantalising mystery.

One day, a week or so after the first glimpse, I was outside with the other helper, doing the washing, casting sly glances across the road as usual. I noticed Jun coming out of the storeroom and my heart quickened. He looked across the street at us and I averted my eyes. My friend leant over and whispered in my ear.

'Look at him,' she giggled. 'He's gorgeous and I think he's looking at me.'

'No,' I said, quite certain that I was right. 'He's definitely looking at me.'

I felt the same shock of excitement as before and concentrated my attention on the washing, keeping my eyes modestly averted as my friend giggled and nudged me embarrassingly.

Every afternoon I had to go to a bakery in town to buy bread for the afternoon tea and next day's breakfast. It was a long walk and so one day I asked Auntie if I could borrow her daughter's bike, as no one was using it.

'It'll mean I get back much faster to start on the meal,' I said, knowing her first thought would be that I was trying to take advantage of her generosity of spirit.

'If you like,' she shrugged, disinterested in how I did my work as long as I did it and cost her as little as possible.

I wheeled the bike out into the street, climbed on, wobbled a little as I got my balance and started to pedal, hoping Jun was watching and would see me sailing elegantly past. I'd only gone a few paces when there was a terrible crunching noise and the pedals spun uselessly beneath my feet. I dismounted and looked down to see the black oily chain hanging loosely in the dust. If I touched that I was likely to get covered in oil and that would not be becoming.

'Do you want me to repair that for you?' a man's voice asked.

I looked up to find myself staring straight into Jun's eyes. 'No,' I stuttered, panic-stricken and blushing. 'I'm all right, thank you.'

'I'll do that for you,' he said, ignoring my protests and bending down to look at the damage.

He was even more handsome close up than he had been from across the street, with the sort of pale skin that Filipino girls love. Just as Western women all want to have tans, Filipinas long to be pale and hide their faces from the sun whenever possible. My heart was thumping again and I was gasping for air as if I was drowning.

'Are you the daughter of that old woman?' he asked casually as he worked on the chain, not seeming to care that the oil was blackening his fingers.

'No,' I managed to reply, 'I only work there. She's my aunt.'

I later found out that he was seven years older than me. He seemed so relaxed and confident, while I was struck almost dumb with a mixture of love and inexperience. It didn't take him long to fit the chain back on and he straightened up to watch as I stammered my thanks and climbed back onto the saddle, praying I would be able to get going without falling off in front of him. I didn't look back as I pedalled away round the corner, only then resting to catch my breath. I couldn't stop myself from grinning like a fool.

Now we had introduced ourselves he smiled and waved every time he saw me across the street. The ice had been broken and now I just had to see what would happen next.

'He was asking me about you,' my fellow helper told me the next day.

'Who?' I asked, although I knew exactly who she meant.

'The handsome man outside, of course,' she tutted as if I was stupid. 'He was saying how pretty you are.'

'Oh, no,' I said, blushing. 'I don't think so.'

She tutted again and raised her eyes as if she despaired of me. Despite my modesty, I was getting used to hearing compliments about my looks from the other staff at the house.

'I remember when you first came to work here,' one

of them had told me. 'You were so cute, but now you have grown up to be beautiful.'

Several of them had said the same thing. It was wonderful to receive such compliments but I never knew how to react. I didn't want anyone to think I was vain about my appearance, but I was pleased by the attention, especially if it was coming from Jun.

He started writing me letters, telling me how much he liked me and inviting me to go with him to a movie. It sounded like the most exciting thing in the world to do. I asked Auntie if that would be possible.

'No.' She was adamant, not even giving the question a moment's consideration. 'You're too young. You're not going anywhere.'

I'd expected that response. She never liked me to go out, even if it was with the other staff. If they were planning to go to the movies or somewhere together and she heard they were intending to take me, she would ask me to stay in and give her a massage instead.

'You give such good massages, Gina,' she'd say, as if I should be flattered to be asked. 'And my old bones ache so at the end of a hard day.'

I never had the nerve to refuse, even when it was the end of a hard day's work for me as well and I knew she hadn't done anything but sit around bossing everyone else about.

Every time I caught a glimpse of Jun outside the warehouse it would make my day perfect. It felt like my insides were melting whenever he smiled at me. I would catch myself staring at him with open-mouthed wonder and have to look away quickly, overwhelmed with confusion.

Sometimes I would steal a few minutes to talk to him as I went to and fro on my various errands, slipping into the storeroom so that Auntie wouldn't spot me and tell me off for wasting time and endangering my reputation. Sometimes he would be drinking with his friends, all of them laughing and joking and teasing one another, which made him seem even more grown-up and exciting to me.

One day he bought me a box of chocolates and waited for me to come back home from the shop where I'd been delivering a meal to the staff. When he presented them to me I was as thrilled as if he was offering a diamond necklace. I'd never been given such a gift before and it made me think that perhaps he felt the same way about me as I did about him, and perhaps it wasn't an impossible dream that we might end up together.

Auntie had spotted my admirer once or twice on her way to and from the shop. It seemed his friendly smile was enough to melt even her frosty heart. She had to admit that he looked 'a nice young man'. I began to wonder if there was a chance that soon she would allow me to go on a date with him.

'Do you have a photograph of yourself?' Jun asked one day when we had a few snatched moments to ourselves.

'Sure,' I said, 'Why?'

'I want to show it to my parents,' he said, grinning and looking deep into my eyes. 'I want them to see how pretty you are, so they will choose you.'

'Choose me?' I didn't understand what he meant, but it sounded very promising.

'There's another girl, who they want me to marry,' he said. 'I want to show them how much prettier you are, so they will change their minds.'

The thought of there being another girl in his life arrived like a knife in my heart, but I loved the idea that he believed I was prettier than her. My mind a blur of conflicting emotions, I ran back to the house and found a photograph that some friend of Auntie's had taken in the dry goods store, which I thought made me look nice. I took it back to him and he examined it closely, exclaiming again at how pretty I was, making me glow with pleasure and forget about the other girl. What chance did she have?

The moment I was back in the house the worries started. What if his parents were too stubborn to change their minds? What if this girl came from a rich family, which could offer him good prospects? My confidence ebbed lower and lower with every passing day.

'I showed your picture to my parents,' he said a few days later, as if it was the most casual announcement in the world.

'What did they say?' I wanted to know.

'They said you were very pretty,' he grinned happily. 'They said they would choose you.'

'Oh.' I didn't know what to say, I couldn't find any words. I just grinned stupidly.

'I love you,' he said, and I felt happier than I'd ever felt in my life.

'Can you take me to meet your parents?' he asked.

'Sure,' I said, trying to sound as casual as him.

I knew his family was better off than mine, and that he was better educated than me, but I had no hesitation in agreeing to take him to the mountain house to meet my parents. In fact I couldn't wait to show him off to them and felt proud to let him see where I came from. I was sure he would love my family as much as I did. He brought his cousin with him on the first visit to make it look more like a social visit. Mum liked him, finding no reason to object to him continuing to court me. At the end of the visit he sat down with her, a serious look on his face.

'I would like to ask your permission to marry your daughter,' he said, very formally.

'Oh my God!' Mum was obviously as shocked as I was. 'But she's too young!'

Jun smiled understandingly and didn't press his case. I guess he wanted her to have time to let the idea sink in. I was beside myself with excitement. All the way back to Sorsogon he and I talked about what we should do and how we could be together. The law in the Philippines was that you couldn't marry until you were 18. I was only just approaching my 17th birthday, but neither of us wanted to have to wait a whole year before dedicating ourselves to one another. We went over and over the options before us but couldn't decide on the right path.

A few days later I received a letter from Jun, delivered by my friend, the cook, telling me he'd been in a fight and had had his face punched.

'Did he give you this letter himself?' I asked her.

'Yes. He looked really bad, Gina, his lip was swollen and cut.' She held her hand up in front of her face, spreading her fingers wide to indicate just how damaged poor Jun was.

The letter explained he was at his family home and asked me to come and see him. It would be an errand of mercy. I told Auntie I was going to see my family because I knew if I told the truth she would not let me go. I hurried over as soon as I'd finished my chores, anxious at what I would find. It was the first time I'd been to the house and I was surprised by how big it was. It belonged to his aunt, who had married well and was living in Switzerland. It was even bigger than the house I'd worked in in Manila.

My next shock was the sight of his face as he opened the door to my knock. His lip was just as swollen as my friend had described, and badly cut, but he seemed not to be bothered, just pleased to see me. He invited me in and introduced me to his cousin and grandma, who were welcoming and kind. They talked politely for a few minutes and then Jun took me to see his room. He closed the door as soon as we were inside and we were finally alone. All he wanted was for me to kiss him.

'I can't kiss you,' I said, half horrified and half laughing. 'Look at your poor lip.'

'It'll make it better,' he teased, trying to smile despite the pain.

I did as he wanted, pressing my lips gently to his, smelling his skin and feeling his soft breath on mine. It was a wonderful feeling. I really, really loved this man. I'd only kissed one boy before, on the cheek. He was a friend, who I'd felt nothing for, and this was a completely different experience, more beautiful than I could ever have imagined. I felt like I was a real woman now, not a little girl any longer.

'I want to marry you as soon as possible,' he said. 'You must talk to your mother and get her permission.'

'She thinks I'm too young,' I said, worried that if I couldn't talk my mother round he might lose patience and go back to the other girl.

'That's why you must talk to her. I'm sure you can change her mind.'

I agreed to do what I could, although I couldn't see how my mother's permission would make any difference to the law. A few days later I persuaded Auntie to let me go back to the mountain house again, carrying in my head a plan.

'I don't want to go on working at Auntie's any more,' I told Mum as we sat drinking coffee in the house.

'So what are you going to do instead?' she asked.

'Well,' I said, thoughtfully, 'I either want to go back to Manila to get a better paid job with some prospects, or to marry Jun. Which would you prefer I did?'

'I don't want you to go anywhere,' she said. 'But you're so young for marriage.'

'It's what I want, Mama,' I insisted.

'Then you must do what you want,' she shrugged. She probably thought that once Jun and I were faced with the difficulties of me being underage we would give up our dream for a year anyway.

'So,' I felt a rush of excitement run through me at her reluctant approval. 'Can I invite his parents here?'

'As you wish, Gina,' she sighed and started talking about something else as if there was nothing more to be said on the subject.

It is the custom in the Philippines when a young couple are courting for the relatives of the boy to visit the relatives of the girl in order to make a presentation, bringing loads of food and drink with them. The idea, I suppose, is for the boy's parents to make a case for why the girl's parents should be honoured to have him as a son-in-law. If everything goes well the two families then eat together, get to know one another, discuss details and set a date for the wedding.

Jun's family made the journey in a jeepney and once the ice had been broken everyone got on well. Watching everyone talking, laughing and drinking happily together seemed to confirm in my mind that I'd found the right man. Even Auntie seemed to approve of my decision and made no fuss when I told her I was going to give up working for her and go back to live with my parents until the wedding.

I was even allowed to sleep over at Jun's house from time to time, although my parents said we were not allowed to have sex, being afraid I might fall pregnant and that Jun would then change his mind. There's still a strong belief in the Philippines that a girl should be a virgin on her wedding night. If she's discovered to have lied the groom is entitled to send her back to her parents the next day, which would bring a terrible disgrace on the family. I knew they were right, but it was hard to stay strong when we were so in love.

Whenever Jun came to our house for the night we would have to wait until all my brothers and my parents were asleep and then we would crawl around the floor to get to one another, just to be close, drawn together like magnets. In the mornings we would have to make sure we were back in our proper beds before anyone else woke up and discovered us entwined in one another's arms.

His parents, however, didn't have any such reservations and made up a double bed for us when we were at their house. I didn't protest but, knowing what he was going to be after, I wore my jeans to bed, doing the belt up really tight.

'Take those off,' he coaxed as he slipped into bed beside me. 'You'll be too hot.'

'No,' I replied, carefully averting my eyes from his. 'I'll be okay.'

When he cuddled me in bed I so much wanted to make love to him, but I knew that if something went wrong it would be me who would be the loser, so I stayed firm and kept his fingers away from my belt buckle.

Although all our parents and relatives were now resigned to the idea of us getting married, there was still the technical problem of me being under 18.

'My father has made a suggestion,' Jun told me one day. 'He says why doesn't he give us some money to run away and live together?'

My future father-in-law was suggesting that he gave us the equivalent of about £200, which is what he would have had to spend on a wedding anyway.

'No,' I said, 'as much as I love you I would rather have my family with me on my wedding day than have the money in my pocket.'

'But we may not be able to marry for over a year,' he protested.

'If you can wait,' I said, 'so can I.'

I was more frightened by my own words than I could allow him to know. What if he couldn't wait? What would I do then? He didn't say anything at the time, but he had a look of determination on his face. A little while later he told me he'd managed to persuade someone working in the local authority to lie about my age on the certificate. I don't know how he did it, but I think it was a favour done by a friend. I didn't cross-examine him, I was just happy to think he loved me enough to have gone to all that trouble to marry me and that soon we would be together all the time.

We were married a year after we first met. All our relatives were there for the celebration, as well as neighbours from both our hometowns. There were around 200 people in all. My family provided two pigs and a hundred kilos of rice, while Jun's family provided two pigs, chickens, fruit and traditional festival dishes like *suman*, which is a sticky rice wrapped in banana leaves, *ibos*, a sticky rice cooked in coconut milk with salt and wrapped in coconut leaves, and *lanson*, a sort of rice cake which is still my favourite. They also supplied an angel cake as the wedding cake.

Both families butchered and prepared the meat together and constructed a *nepar* (grass reed) roof suspended on bamboo legs, which was about 40 feet long and 30 feet wide. The feast took place the night before the wedding, starting at six in the evening and continuing until everyone had gone to bed at midnight. At six the next morning we were up again having breakfast. The immediate family went to the church for the ceremony while the other guests carried on eating. I wore a traditional long white dress, with a tiara and a veil and Jun wore black trousers and a *baron tagalog*, a traditional men's wedding suit. The ceremony we had was known as a 'special wedding', which Jun's family had asked for and meant we had a red carpet leading us into the church and they had arranged flowers on the way to the altar.

Jun and all our close relations waited inside the church for Papa to lead me in. Jun looked so handsome as he turned to watch me coming through the door and I felt I was the most beautiful bride who had ever lived. I was so proud for my family to see me dressed so beautifully and marrying such a man.

After the ceremony we went back to the house just in time for lunch and the party continued with everybody eating and drinking all through the day and night. Once it was all over I collapsed into bed, sick from the stress of all the preparation and excitement.

We went back to live at his mother's house once we were married, which is the tradition for young couples. Jun's family had moved out of his aunt's house by that time so that it could be renovated for her to come back to. Although their own house was not as big as his aunt's, it was still very nice. It was in the countryside, on the family's farmland. They were a traditional farming family like mine, but they were more comfortably off because many of the family members were living and working abroad, sending back money. That was still what I wanted to do for my family, even though my plans had been delayed by falling in love.

At last Jun and I were free to make love, but on the first night after the wedding we were both too exhausted and fell asleep before anything happened. The next morning Jun's father reminded me I should wash in warm water after losing my virginity. I didn't tell him that nothing had changed.

We made love a few times in the coming weeks but Jun couldn't understand why I didn't bleed. Nor could I.

'How come you aren't a virgin?' he asked.

'I don't know,' I said. 'I never slept with any men.'

He was more experienced than me, having had a girlfriend before, and I didn't really know what to expect. I liked making love, even though it hurt a lot, but I couldn't explain why I wasn't bleeding. I was terrified that he might decide he had made a mistake and send me back home in disgrace, but he didn't say anything and I avoided the subject at all costs. After three weeks, when I was sitting on top of him for the first time during sex, the blood came and I was no longer a virgin. It was a big shock, but an even bigger relief. After that it didn't hurt to make love any more and I was able to enjoy sex without any anxiety, like any other young bride.

All through my childhood I'd been working, seldom able to relax for more than a few minutes, almost never getting as much sleep as a growing child needs, even though it hadn't felt like work for the first few years. The stress must have been building inside my head for a long time.

I guess I was constantly overtired but I was so used to the feeling it seemed normal, and I was always on edge from worrying about my family. Being married to Jun, at last I had someone to take care of me, someone to love me, someone of my own. Perhaps that made me relax and then the stresses that I had been holding back for so long began to overwhelm me. Almost as soon as we were married I started to develop strange symptoms. I was shaking all the time. It was a difficult adjustment, but it wasn't enough of a problem to affect my happiness at being with Jun and being able to lie safely in his arms at night.

Within a couple of months of the wedding I discovered I was pregnant. I was so happy to think we would be having a child together, a product of our love, but I started getting pains in my stomach. I went to see the doctor, but he couldn't find anything wrong.

I gave birth to my daughter, Dailyn, at my mother-in-law's house, with the help of a local nurse. I felt so proud to be holding my baby girl. A couple of days later Dailyn turned yellow. Jun rushed her to the hospital, but I didn't have the strength to go with her, having just given birth. I was feeling very ill indeed. It was as if some evil spirit was taking over both my mind and my body. Just when everything should have been perfect, things felt as if they were starting to go wrong; no one could possibly have foreseen just how badly wrong everything was about to become.

CHAPTER FIVE

Possessed by Devils

Although we were a Catholic family, like many in the Philippines, we still believed in some of the old superstitions that haunted our islands for many centuries before the Spanish first arrived to conquer and convert our ancestors.

People who live for generations in the jungle have their own beliefs about the spirits and devils that inhabit the shadows beneath the trees and haunt the hot, humid air. There has to be some other explanation apart from 'God's will' for all the terrible things that happen in a land so often plagued by volcanoes, earthquakes and typhoons. How could it be possible that the all-loving Christian God could do anything as cruel as sending a giant wave to sweep away the home of an honest, god-fearing family like ours? It had to be the work of a more malign force.

As small children we were told the same ancient tales as our parents and grandparents had been told when they were young, and it's impossible to completely

shake off such deeply rooted beliefs when they are plant-
ed in young enough minds, even for those lucky enough
to enjoy a long education. Faith healers and witch doctors
are still prevalent in the islands and their explanations
and cures often seem as likely to be right as any that
Western religions or modern science can think up.
Everyone wants to find believable explanations for unbe-
lievable events.

If the doctors in the hospital could come up with no
explanation, even with all their machines and sophisti-
cated drugs, as to why I was so sick and growing sicker
by the day, then it seemed possible there must be some
other causes beyond their comprehension, something
altogether darker and more mysterious.

Before I met Jun there had been a man working in
Auntie's shop who fell in love with me, or so he said. He
wanted me to go out with him, but I told him it wasn't
possible because I didn't fancy him and it seemed unkind
to encourage him and get his hopes up. One day he took
a photograph of me and I thought nothing of it since
there were other people around at the time and it was
done in good spirit. He never showed me the picture
he'd taken and I forgot all about the incident.

A little while later I woke up in the middle of the
night with a really itchy face. It grew worse and I crept
to the bathroom, as quietly as I could so as not to wake
the others living in Auntie's house, and switched on the
light. My face was so swollen I couldn't even open my

eyes properly. I squinted into the mirror, taking a few seconds to work out whose distorted reflection I was looking at. My face was all puffy and red and my neck was almost as thick as my head. The itching made me want to rip my skin off.

The next day everyone was as shocked as I had been to see the change in me. Auntie's husband tried all sorts of Chinese remedies in an attempt to stop the itching and bring down the swelling. When none of them worked he took me into hospital and they gave me an anti-allergy cream. Nothing seemed to have any effect and the condition continued for almost five months. In the end I had virtually no skin left on my face and neck. I was in despair. A faith healer came to see me at Auntie's house.

'This is the work of black magic,' he said as soon as he saw the state of my face.

'Black magic?' I was shocked. 'Who would do such a thing?'

'Has anyone else mentioned black magic since this happened to you?' he asked.

I thought back and remembered the man who had asked me out being the only one to have mentioned black magic to me in relation to my ailments. I told the faith healer.

'Then he's the one who's done this,' the healer said. 'Could you have offended him?'

'I didn't think I had,' I replied. 'But he did ask me out and I said no.'

'Ah,' the healer nodded sagely as if this explained everything. 'Does he have a photograph of you?'

'Yes, he did take one,' I said, remembering the fact for the first time in ages. 'But I never saw it. I don't even know if it came out.'

'Then that is the answer,' the healer said.

I was shocked and frightened by what he was suggesting. Now I thought about it I could remember times when the man had acted oddly around me, but I'd just thought it was part of his personality and had taken no notice. The thought of him deliberately putting a curse on me made me shiver. Somewhere he must have that photograph and be doing horrible things to it, imagining he was doing them to me. It felt like my body and mind had been invaded by an invisible enemy. Nothing was safe; there was nowhere I could hide, not even in my own thoughts.

'So what happens now?' I wanted to know.

'You will get better,' the healer assured me.

He then started his healing process, laying his hands on my face and neck. To my horror a swarm of tiny ants came crawling to the surface of my skin as if panicked into breaking cover.

'Where have they come from?' I screamed, frantically trying to brush them away.

'They have been living beneath your skin, eating your flesh,' he explained.

'How did they get there?'

'Your enemy must have put them there with a curse.'

When he'd finished rooting out the demons and the last of the ants had been chased away, the healer wrote down a formula, transferring his power onto a piece of paper and giving it to me.

'Keep that for the rest of your life,' he said, 'or you will become very, very ill. You will get terrible stomach pains if you don't look after it.'

Such beliefs seem foolish in the light of Western science and medicine, I know. But when you've been in so much distress for so long and a man gives you an explanation and a cure, and his explanation fits in with much of the folklore you were brought up to believe, things seem different. No one at the hospital had told me there was a colony of ants living under my skin. The healer had been the only one able to offer any sort of cure. Why should I not believe him?

For ages I kept that written formula, but then, once I was used to feeling well again, I became careless and I lost it. During my pregnancy with Dailyn, the stomach pains started, just as he had predicted. I was going in and out of hospital having tests, but no doctors could give me any explanation as to why I felt so weak and sick all the time.

Lying in bed in my husband's family home, unable to raise enough energy to even look after my beautiful newborn child, let alone work in the house, I began to miss my parents and my brothers and sisters. I'd been separated from them for so much of my life and now I was separated from them again, even though I loved Jun and was happy to be married to him; even though I had a baby girl whom I adored. My mind kept working, churning over thoughts and feelings that I couldn't control. Everything seemed black and threatening and hopeless. I could see no way out of the pit that I was falling into.

Jun's parents suggested we build a house close to theirs, which was the traditional way for a young couple to live, but in my heart I wanted to be closer to my own family. It was as if I needed to make up for all the years I'd been apart from them when I was a child. But I didn't have the strength to fight very hard for what I wanted, and I don't think I could have won anyway because tradition is a powerful force. So soon we were building a little house near to my parents-in-law, even though my heart wasn't in it. More than anything I wanted to please Jun and be with him and Dailyn, so I didn't protest, but I couldn't imagine living there for the rest of my life.

Jun's parents had a duck farm on their land and they suggested that our house was built there and we could look after the business, going halves on anything that it earned. The house was only wood and was built very quickly. We lived close to the banks of the river where the ducks lived, surrounded by tall palm trees which made it appear dark even when the sun was streaming in. Every morning it was exciting to find the eggs along the banks or in the water. Every day we were able to eat them freshly scrambled. It would have been an idyllic life if I hadn't been feeling so ill and so homesick.

One night Dailyn and I were alone in the house in bed together while Jun was out drinking with his friends. They drank quite a lot together now. Perhaps they always had and I just knew nothing about it. I didn't like it when he was out at night. I wanted us to be a family together. I wanted to feel his arms around me as I cuddled Dailyn.

I was trying to coax her to take some milk when every hair on my skin stood on end. Outside the stillness of the night was shattered by an explosion of quacking from the ducks. I could hear heavy footsteps walking around the building. My heart was thumping in my chest. I was terrified Dailyn would start to cry and attract whoever it was into the house. I froze in the bed, nursing her for as long as I could to keep her quiet. Seconds dragged past like hours and soon the tension of not knowing what was happening in the darkness outside was too much to bear. Carefully laying my baby down on the bed, I got up and walked to the door.

'Jun?' I called out, surprised by how small my voice sounded. 'Are you there?'

There was no reply and my fears overcame me. I started to scream, hoping the family would be able to hear me all the way up at the main house.

'Mama! Mama!' I shrieked, like a lost and panic-stricken child.

I could hear them calling back. 'Gina? Are you okay?'

'No,' I shouted and they came hurrying down with lanterns to see what the matter was.

'I'm so frightened,' I told them, comforted just to have other people around. 'I heard footsteps and the ducks were all quacking.'

They managed to calm me down to wait for Jun and went back to the house. I kept straining my ears and imagining I could hear rustlings in the silence of the night. Jun eventually stumbled home at about midnight, having had too much gin to be able to understand what I was trying to tell him through my garbled sobbing. From then on I hated being alone in the house at night and cried a lot, desperately trying not to convey my fears to my baby.

'Why don't you take Gina home,' I heard my mother-in-law telling Jun one day. 'I think she's missing her family.'

Being increasingly worried about my state of mind, he took her advice and Dailyn and I stayed with my parents for a while. I felt a bit more relaxed when I was at home with Mum and living amongst my own family, not having to put on a show as the dutiful daughter-in-law all the time, but still the pains that had plagued me all through my pregnancy in my stomach, and the black cloud in my brain, wouldn't go away.

Although I was married to the man I adored, and although I had a baby who was perfect in every way, I felt I was crying inside and I had no idea why, or what to do to stop the feeling.

In the West the doctors would probably have been diagnosing post-natal depression, but I knew nothing of such things. All I knew was that it felt like I had a thousand demons screaming inside my head, telling me I was a bad daughter, wife and mother and that there was no hope of things ever getting better. I couldn't hope to ask Jun's parents for help, but I did hope I might be able to go to Mum. It was harder than I expected to bring the subject up. I kept trying to pluck up the courage and then failing.

'Mama,' I eventually asked her one day, while we were washing the clothes together in the river, 'how do you cope with all the problems and pains of life?'

She straightened up from her work, pressing her hand into the small of her back to ease the aching.

'Oh, Gina,' she said, half smiling and half sad, 'now I know you are a woman. I remember when you were tiny and asked me where problems come from and how you could get one. Now you know the answer to that question. What's wrong with you?'

I looked at her and opened my mouth to talk but the words wouldn't come. I searched in my head for some sort of explanation as to how I was feeling and why I was so unhappy and could find nothing. There was no reason and no logic. There was just the pain and the sadness, yet I had everything a woman could want in life, so why did I feel like this?

'I'm not well at all,' was all I said.

Mama waited for a few moments and when nothing more came from my lips she gave a little nod, as if this confirmed something that she, as an older woman, could more than understand, and went back to her work without saying another word. I watched her for a moment, angry with her for not trying harder to find out what was wrong with her daughter and angry with myself for not being able to find the words she needed to hear; then I bent down and went back to work beside her.

A little later, as we were making our way up to the house with the wet washing dripping in our arms, she spoke again.

'There's a faith healer I know,' she said. 'I'll take you to see him.'

The next day we went to see the man, who looked deep into my eyes and ran his hands over my body, before pronouncing that the problem lay with my appendix. That, he said, was why I was suffering from stomach pains.

'It will get better,' he assured us both. 'You need to give it time.'

Jun came up to the house later that day and we sat down to talk. I told him what the healer had said.

'You need to go to hospital,' Jun said. 'We must find out what is wrong with you once and for all. If it is your appendix they can operate on it.'

'What about Dailyn?' I asked, worried about leaving my mother with yet another child to look after.

'We can take her to my parents,' Jun said.

'I don't know,' I said. 'I have to think about it.'

I was frightened because the first faith healer had told me that the black magic curse put on me by the man in Auntie's shop would be even more infuriated by the sight of a hospital. That night I had what must have been a sort of panic attack; I was hardly able to breathe. They tried to revive me in the traditional way by smacking my arms and legs, but I wasn't able to feel the blows. It was as if I was too far away from reality to feel anything physical, like I'd been given an anaesthetic. The next morning I couldn't remember what had happened from the way the others described it to me; it was as if my memory had been wiped clean of those hours. I was confused and angry, still panicking and struggling for breath. They told me I must go into hospital, just as Jun had said, and I did as I was told, but I was fighting and punching anyone who came near me. I don't remember any of this; I only know what my family have told me since.

Once they got me to the hospital the black magic took a terrible hold of my brain. I cried all the time, wandering around the building talking to every stranger

I came across, all inhibitions gone. The doctors put me on a drip and told me they would do ultrasound tests the next day. They expected me to go to sleep, but I just kept talking to everyone, picking arguments. I pulled the drips out and announced I wanted to leave, walking to the door. I didn't want to go back to Jun's house because I knew he would take me back to the hospital, so I went to my sister Beth's home. That was when something must have exploded in my brain.

There was a knife in Beth's kitchen and apparently I grabbed it and started to chase people around, including Beth and Mum, driven by the demons in my head. Everyone was screaming and running away. Someone went to fetch Jun, believing he was the only person who might be able to control me. When he arrived he tried to calm me, but the demons must have been raging so violently inside me by then that I couldn't hear any reason, not even when it was voiced by the man I loved.

We were outside the house, standing in the street, everyone hiding away from me, watching to see what would happen, poised to run if I came at them. Jun must have tried to get the knife away from me before I did any more damage, but I was too wild to control and lashed out, stabbing him in the stomach. He pulled away from me and stumbled off, shouting for someone to get him to the hospital. I'm told I kept chasing everyone I could see, like a child playing a deadly game of tag.

Eventually I was persuaded to drop the knife and the other family members managed to get Jun to the hospital. Everyone was running around, worried and not knowing what to do. The doctors told them there was a 50 per cent chance they would be unable to save his life.

My dad, who'd been fetched from the mountains to take charge of the situation, had to go to Jun's parents' house to inform them what a terrible thing his daughter had done. When they saw him coming from the window they assumed he was bringing news of the ultrasound test the doctors had said they would do on me, and they welcomed him into the house, anxious to find out what was wrong with the daughter-in-law they'd chosen for their beloved son.

Dad was deeply shamed by what I'd done. Being a proud and honourable man he was determined to make amends to Jun's family in any way he could. He insisted he would pay for Jun's expenses in the hospital, but to honour that promise he had to sell the family's carabaw and a large part of our land in the mountains. It was all he had to give in recompense for the harm his youngest daughter had inflicted on them. He was in despair. Jun's father came to see me and I'm told I clung to him, begging him to take me to the hospital to see Jun.

'No,' he insisted, 'you're not going anywhere. The best thing you can do for me, and for Jun, is to get better yourself.'

★

But I didn't get better. In fact things grew worse as the madness took hold. The doctors said there was nothing wrong with my appendix, that all the problems were in my head. My behaviour became worse and worse as I travelled further from sanity and reality. I would rip off my clothes and go naked, not caring who saw me. I would wet myself without even seeming to notice. It was obvious to everyone that I couldn't care for Dailyn while I was out of my mind, that I might actually be a danger to her, so my parents-in-law said they would look after her. They were right. If I was able to stab the man I adored, what terrible thing might I do to my baby while in the grip of some delusion?

I went back to the house in the mountains and my parents, while Jun recovered in the hospital and my father worked to recompense his family. Sometimes in my delirium I would escape from whoever was supposed to be watching me and turn up at the hospital, demanding to see my husband, but the medical staff wouldn't let me in.

My mother brought every faith healer she could find to the house to try to drive the spirits out of me. She and my father didn't want to take me back to hospital because they were sure that was what had made the curse so active. Even in the safety of my family home I grew worse. I didn't bother with eating, unable to care enough to lift food to my mouth. I became thinner, weaker and more lethargic until the skin was just hanging on my bones, all the flesh gone. I lay around all day, unable to find a reason to stand up.

'It would be better for her to die than to go on suffering like this,' my parents both said as they despaired of me ever regaining my strength.

'I want to get better,' I would tell them in the brief moments when I was speaking coherently, repeating the mantra over and over. 'There must be someone I can go to. I just want to disappear and come back cured.'

But they'd spent so much money looking after Jun in hospital that anything else they managed to save had to be for the rest of the family. They couldn't afford to spend any more on me, so there was nothing they could do. I was a lost cause. My father became exasperated. Worn down by hard work and exhaustion, seeing no end to the toil and worry, he would boil over with anger at the end of each day, telling me I was useless and lazy. He couldn't understand why I wasn't able to find the energy to do anything to help myself. I just sat around the house, watching the world through blank eyes, often not bothering to put on clothes and soiling myself wherever I was. I stank of dirt and excrement.

One day, while my father was out working in the mountains, something snapped inside my head again and I started chasing everyone around the house with a machete. I hit my brother on the head as he tried to run away. Then I turned on Mum, slashing into the back of her neck with the heavy blade.

Other family members, including my grandfather, heard the commotion and came running to the house to help disarm me, restrain me and settle me down. Mum had to be rushed to hospital. Her life was saved, but the scar would be there for the rest of her life to remind me that yet again I had turned on one of the people who loved me the most.

Once my mother had been taken into the care of the doctors, my grandfather's biggest worry was what my father would do to me when he got home and discovered I'd attacked his wife and son. He knew Dad was already near the edge and furious with me for destroying the family and Granddad thought he too might snap on receiving this piece of news. Once everything had been taken care of at the house, Granddad hurried up into the mountains to look for Dad. He found him working on the land and gently took his machete away from him before he told him what had happened. By the time the two men came back from the mountains the rest of the family were all around me, trying to comfort and protect me as I raved and wept uncontrollably.

My grandfather had been wise to take the machete away from my father. His anger and frustration were so great he attacked me with his fists, punching me all over my body in a hopeless, uncontrollable rage. When the others managed to pull him off me, he sent for the police and demanded that they take me away and lock me up, saying the family couldn't be expected to watch over me every hour of the day any more. But the policemen just shook their heads and shrugged; perhaps they had seen such scenes of domestic horror too many times.

'We can't put her in prison,' they said. 'She's mentally ill.'

'But she could kill us all in her madness,' Dad insisted. 'She has attacked her husband, her brother, her mother, which of us will be next? Do we have to wait until she kills someone before we are protected from her?'

'We don't think she will do that,' they replied, climbing back into their car and driving away, leaving him in despair.

He went to the mental hospital to get me admitted, and the doctors there said they would take me, but he then decided not to risk putting me there in case I got pregnant with one of the other inmates. I was taking no pride in myself and might easily have let the men have their way with me, not caring, or maybe not even noticing, like I didn't care or notice when I soiled myself.

'We'll keep her at home,' he decided eventually, once he'd calmed down and my mother's condition had stabilised in the hospital. 'But we must lock her up so that she's not a danger to the rest of us.'

Getting out his carpentry tools he brought lumber down from the mountain and built a box-like extension to the kitchen area of the house. It was just big enough for me to lie down on the floor, like a kennel for a dog that is too ferocious and unreliable to be allowed to roam free. I stayed in the box most of the time. It sounds terrible but as I can't remember any of it maybe it made no difference to me where I was. If I needed to come out to be washed they would chain my hands or my legs.

Because I wasn't bothering to feed myself my brothers used to do it for me, like they would have done for a baby: patiently lifting the food to my lips and encouraging me to chew and swallow, trying to get some nourishment into my pathetic little frame. Once she was allowed out of hospital, my mother was understandably terrified to be near me and so her sister would wash and bathe me when I became too filthy and smelt too strongly for them to be able to stand it in the house a moment longer.

As well as turning to faith healers for help, my mother also tried to enlist the assistance of the Catholic God. When my father was a little boy he fell very ill and his family took him to a church that was famous for answering the prayers of anyone who needed healing. Those who were cured would promise to go back to the church regularly for the rest of their lives to give thanks. Dad had always kept his childhood promise and had brought us all up to do the same. Every year, whether we could afford the trip or not, we would all take the three-hour bus ride there to show our gratitude to God for sparing our father.

During her search for a cure for my affliction, Mum took me there. The priest anointed me with sacred oil as

I sat before him, weak and shivering, but still the curse wouldn't lift. She had one last faith healer to call on and had resigned herself to the fact that if this one didn't manage to save me I would die because there would be nothing more she could do. The man came back and forth to the house several times to see me and never asked them for any money, giving them a mixture of herbs which he told them to grind down into tea for me.

'We can make your daughter better,' he assured her. She was going to need a lot of faith to believe that after so long.

Eighteen months after I first ran amok with the knife at Beth's house, the demons left me in the night, just as suddenly as they had arrived. It was like waking up from a long sleep, filled with troubling dreams you can't quite remember. I found myself covered in filth, my hair matted and my body like a skeleton. It was confusing and no matter how hard I concentrated I wasn't able to piece together what had happened to me to have ended up locked in a box in such terrible conditions.

Everyone could see that the blackness had passed like storm clouds in the wind and that my senses had returned. Over the coming months different people would tell me different things that had happened and that I had done during that year and a half in the darkness and I was able to piece together a picture. Every time I gave my mother a massage I could see the ugly scar across the back of her neck where I'd struck her with the machete. I could so easily have woken from my sleep to find I'd killed my own mother as well as my husband.

As quickly as the madness lifted the guilt descended like a curtain. I could see that instead of helping my parents, as I'd always sworn I would do, I'd actually made their lives a hundred times worse. I'd cost them almost every spare penny they had and made them more vulnerable than ever. I thought they must hate me so much and I could understand why.

None of Dad's family wanted to come near me because they said I still smelled so bad. Having not looked after myself for so many months I'd become a frightening sight and no one wanted me near their children in case my mind slipped again without warning. I was an outcast and I knew I was going to have to work hard to win back their love and respect. I was going to have to find a way of proving myself all over again.

When I was told what I'd done to Jun, the man I loved so much, I couldn't believe it was possible. The thought that I could have hurt him in any way was unbearable. They said that all the time I was sick I'd been saying I wanted to have him and Dailyn back. Now I was recovered and regaining my strength, I longed to be given another chance to be a good wife and mother, like I'd dreamed of being before the demons attacked.

'Don't worry about Dailyn,' Mum said whenever I asked. 'She's being looked after well. One day you'll have another child and you'll be able to forget about her.'

I didn't understand her words. Forget about her? How could I ever forget about Dailyn? She and Jun were my life and now I was being told I could never have them back?

Initially I wanted to sleep all the time. The madness and the prolonged starvation had drained my body and my energies and I needed to rebuild them. Once she had grown used to the idea that I had returned to her, Mum would become exasperated when she couldn't get me out of bed in the mornings to help with the chores.

'Come on, do something,' she would chide me. 'You're lazy and useless. You do nothing but sleep.'

Her words cut me like knives. I'd always worked hard and I'd always had such wonderful dreams of how I would support my family and give them better lives, and all they saw was someone 'lazy and useless' who'd cost them every penny of their meagre savings.

My sisters were all married with children by then, leading lives very similar to our mother's. Beth's husband Josie had treated her badly and they were separated. They had always seemed to be arguing, although I never really understood what it was about, just that it had made my father furious. So when one of our cousins came to visit from Manila, where he worked as a taxi driver, and asked if any of us would like to go to the city to work for him and his wife as a maid, Beth said she would go. This cousin owned some of the land near to ours and Dad would look after it for him, so sometimes he would come to visit in order to get his share of the money. Wanting to find a way of re-starting my life and earning some money, I said I would go with her. Beth could have the job working for our cousin and his family and I would find another job once I arrived in the city. Beth had a small daughter and a new baby, who she was going to leave with Mum. Her husband hadn't even known she was pregnant with the second child when they separated. She had always been a headstrong character and a hard worker. She was slim and, although she had a very dark skin, she had a beautiful complexion and a peach-shaped face. I respected and loved her greatly.

Since I couldn't be with Jun and Dailyn, I thought I might as well follow my second chosen path of going to the city and trying to make some of the money I now felt I owed the family. I wanted to escape from the terrible feelings of guilt that weighed me down every time I looked at my parents and saw them struggling through their endless chores from the moment they woke up to the moment they fell asleep.

On the day we were due to leave, my father and mother were working up in the mountains, so I left them a note.

I'm very sorry for what happened. You know I would never hurt you in any way if I could help it. I'm sorry I have caused so much pain and cost you so much money. I will repay you, whatever happens.
Gina.

I left the mountain, carrying all the pain with me. I knew that even if they missed me a little, they would be relieved they had one less burden to shoulder, and I was determined to make them proud of me.

Chapter Six

Making Amends

Beth and I travelled on the bus together. Although she knew where she was going, I had no idea what might lie ahead of me. She had left the children behind with my mother, intending to set up a home in Manila before going back to fetch them. As the hours droned past on the journey, taking me further and further from Jun and Dailyn, I became increasingly nervous, wondering if I'd done the right thing and whether I'd be able to cope away from home again. I snuggled close to my sister and closed my eyes. I remembered how homesick I'd become the last time I was in the Manila and I feared the feeling would return.

As we came into the outskirts of the city, the sight of the busy streets and buildings brought back more memories. I felt excited at what big city adventures might come my way, and yet apprehensive at the same time. I was impatient to find a way to start making money so I could prove to my parents that I wasn't 'useless' and 'lazy', but I didn't want to leave Beth's side. She seemed so strong and certain of her future, and she was my only link with my childhood and with everything that was familiar and safe.

Not yet ready to go anywhere on my own, I followed Beth to our cousin's house. I explained I needed a job and he said he would ask around to see if he could find anyone in the neighbourhood who was looking for a maid. It didn't take him long to come up with a possible family, just a couple of doors away from his house. I went to see them and they said they would love to employ me, but I was shocked to find I couldn't bear the thought of being even that far away from Beth. All the confidence that had carried me to Manila on my own when I was 11 seemed to have deserted me now I was an adult.

'It's only two houses away,' Beth pointed out, puzzled by my reluctance to accept a good offer from people who seemed like a nice family. 'I would still be able to see you every day.'

'I know,' I said, feeling stupid even as I tried to explain. 'But I want to be able to look out the window and see where you are while I'm working. I don't want to be with people I don't know.'

Beth, knowing I must still be in a fragile state of mind, was very understanding and asked our cousin to make more enquiries. To my relief he managed to persuade a widow lady who lived next door with her two grown-up sons to take me on. She was willing to pay the equivalent of nearly a pound a week, four times as much as Auntie had paid me. It was more than I needed to live on and would mean I would have spare money to send home. Knowing I would be able to see Beth whenever I wanted calmed me down, and I agreed to take the job.

I was a good worker and did everything my new boss asked of me, including the laundry, cooking and cleaning. Because they were only a small family it was a light workload compared to what I'd had to do at Auntie's, but in my heart I still yearned to be with Beth all the time. Even though my boss gave me a bedroom of my own, at night I would return to my cousin's house so I could sleep with my sister. I didn't want to be alone in the dark hours in case the demons came back to haunt me.

The widow and her sons were all very kind to me, but my health was still not good. My eyes and my skin turned yellow and however much I ate I didn't seem to be able to regain much of the weight I'd lost during my 18 months of madness. My boss became so concerned about me she asked one of her sons to take me to the hospital for a check-up.

'I don't want to go,' I said, remembering how badly my demons had reacted the last time. 'I'll be okay.'

'But we need to find out what's wrong with you,' he said, kindly but firmly. 'We have good doctors in Manila.'

I didn't put up much of a fight, half of me knowing he was right and I shouldn't be afraid. Part of my brain told me that all the beliefs of my youth were no more than superstitions, but the other part couldn't quite find the courage to dismiss them completely. As long as I even half believed in them, the demons still had the power to influence and frighten me. I plucked up my courage and let him take me.

There was no sign of the demons as I went into the hospital, passing through waiting rooms into consulting rooms and finally undergoing tests. The doctors told me I had a liver problem and gave me some medicine which cleared it up. Maybe, I thought, things were going to be okay. Maybe the demons had finally been defeated.

My boss and her family were so sweet to me, telling me they wanted to adopt me and make me part of their family. It was comforting to believe someone loved me after what I'd been through. It had felt like I'd lost all my family's love over the previous months and it had left a terrible void in my heart.

Despite my boss' kindness I would always go back to Beth the moment I finished my work, or whenever I had a break. Sometimes I would hear the widow calling me from next-door, not realising I wasn't in the house, and I would have to hurry back. She wanted to have me around all the time because she became lonely when her sons were out working or with their girlfriends and there was no one else there. As she was getting older she wanted me to sleep in the house in case she needed help in the night. It was perfectly reasonable for her to ask and I wanted to be able to help, but I still couldn't bear being away from Beth. I felt guilty again, just as I'd felt guilty about my parents, and torn in my loyalties. I was puzzled by the strength of my own fears.

My cousin's wife was also becoming a bit annoyed with me always being in their house, eating their food and taking up Beth's time. Now that my health was improving I'd started eating a lot, building up my strength, which meant I was costing them extra money.

'You must tell her to sleep and take her meals over there,' she told Beth. 'It's no good her coming round here all the time.'

Beth passed the instruction on but I ignored it. The feeling of wanting to be with my sister was stronger than any respect I might have had for my cousin and his wife.

We hadn't been in the city long before Beth's husband, Josie, heard she was there and came looking for her. He came to the house and they sat down to talk. He told her he realised he'd made a mistake in allowing the marriage to fall apart and that he wanted to get back together with her and their daughter as a family. When he found out there was another child that he knew nothing about he was even more determined to persuade her he'd mended his ways and would now be a good father and husband. After Josie had gone Beth came to look for me.

'I've decided to go back to him,' she said.

'But what will Dad say?' I asked.

I was horrified and I knew Dad would be furious.

'Please,' she begged, 'you mustn't tell him.'

I promised I would say nothing. I could understand why she would want to take the risk of going back to Josie if it meant she could bring her children to Manila and have them with her. Beth would then give up her job and they would live together as a family. I would have done almost anything to have been able to have Jun and Dailyn back in my life. I'd actually written Jun a letter, apologising for what had happened, telling him how much I missed him and asking if we could start again. Every day I would watch for the postman, waiting for his reply, praying he would write, saying he felt the same and asking me to go back home.

When his response finally came I opened the envelope with trembling hands, hardly able to breathe, just like I used to feel when I first met him and had no idea whether he felt the same way about me as I did about him. I scanned through the letter, trying to take it all in, trying not to panic until I was sure I'd understood everything he was saying. But certain phrases kept jumping off the page at me.

Forget about our relationship. Forget about us. If you really love your daughter, just try to support her.

His words seemed so final, as if I was never going to see either of them again. If the only way I could stay in contact with Dailyn was to send money to help support her, then I had to find ways of doing that to the best of my ability. I didn't like the idea of staying in my job if Beth wasn't living next door and I couldn't be with her whenever I wasn't working, so I was already thinking about other things I might do to earn extra money and hoping that once they were settled I might be able to move in with Beth and Josie. I knew I had to be strong and start to stand on my own two feet.

Josie's family all lived in Manila. When I went with Beth to meet them, his mother and two of her daughters were talking about jobs. I told them I was trying to think of ways to earn some money to send home to support the family.

'I would like to introduce you to someone I know,' Josie's mother said. 'You would be able to earn much more money than working as a maid.'

'What type of job would it be?' I asked.

'Don't worry about it,' she said. 'You'll earn plenty of money. You'll be able to help your family.'

'That's all I want,' I agreed.

We caught a bus to a part of the city I'd never been to before and she introduced me to a pleasant middle-aged woman with a family, who made me feel very welcome in her home. Being amongst friendly people made me less fearful of my new life. I felt I could trust them to look after me and make sure I didn't get lost or hurt, especially as I'd come to them through Beth. I suddenly felt I was part of a family again.

'I'm going to leave you two together,' Beth's mother-in-law said after we had been talking for a while. 'You can stay here for a few days and see how you get on.'

It was all so friendly I didn't want to ask too many questions. I assumed that perhaps this woman needed a maid and wanted to see what I was like before making a decision, but no one asked me to do any chores. Their family life went on around me and I joined in as much as I could. I was anxious about the future, but felt proud of myself for being able to manage without Beth, even though I was missing her and feeling sad.

After a couple of days the woman said, 'So, do you think you would like the job?'

'What job is this?' I asked.

'It's in a nightclub.'

I'd never been in a bar or a nightclub in my life and had no idea what such a job would entail, but I'd heard tales from other girls returning home from Manila that made me uneasy. I heard about girls being forced into prostitution and made to take drugs. Everyone in the villages always seemed to know of someone who had had something terrible happen to them while away in the big city, although I never personally met anyone who had had that bad a time. Most girls just talked about how much money they'd been able to make and the wonderful places they'd seen. I guess the bad stories flourished because there were people who liked the idea that bar girls would be punished for their 'sins'.

'What would I be doing?' I asked nervously. 'Would I have to be naked?'

Even though I'd been told how I'd sat around naked all the time during my illness, I hadn't been conscious of what I was doing and I had been with my family. I didn't like the idea of taking my clothes off in front of other people now that my inhibitions had returned to normal.

'No,' she replied, avoiding my eyes. 'You just need to dance. You will have beautiful costumes.'

'I like dancing to a record player,' I said, doubtfully. 'But I can't do it properly. How would I do that?'

'You'll be trained by a professional dancer,' she assured me. 'You'll be okay.'

'Do you work in this club then?' I asked.

'Yes,' she nodded. 'I sell flowers to the customers to give to their lady friends, to show how romantic they are.'

'Okay,' I said, 'if you think I would be all right.'

The next day, after a nervous night spent trying to imagine what would be asked of me, my new friend took me to a club called Jools in the centre of the city. It was a big club, one of the best in Manila, she said, catering for all the rich male foreign tourists who stayed in the big hotels. A neon outline of a naked girl advertised the entrance. I was taken to a room and introduced to an Australian couple and told that they were the owners. They were friendly and professional in their manner, but when the woman asked me to take my clothes off a cold chill ran through me. I had imagined they would want to see my figure, but it still came as a shock when they actually asked me to undress. I wanted to run away but had no idea where I would run to. I didn't know the part of town we had come to and I had no money to hire a taxi to take me back to Beth's house, even if I'd known her address.

'We need to see your body to know if you'll be able to dance,' the Australian woman explained.

'Do I have to?' I asked, my voice cracking and tears welling in my eyes.

'Yes,' she said. 'It's important because in some dances you might need to go topless.'

My first thought was that I had a mark round my waist where my mother always tied a piece of string for luck. I'd taken it off the day before, when I'd been told that I would be wearing costumes, but the mark hadn't yet faded and I was embarrassed to have anyone see it. They were obviously serious about me taking my clothes off and I felt that now I'd got this far it would be stupid to refuse and make a scene. This was the only opportunity I'd been offered to make some money. If I ran away now I might never be offered another chance, so I undressed down to my bra and pants, trying to make it look as if I did such things all the time. I felt vulnerable and shaky and the tears were running down my cheeks, but I forced myself to stand in front of them and let them look for as long as they needed.

'What's that around your waist?' the woman asked.

'It's where I had a piece of string,' I explained. 'It's left a mark. I'm sorry.'

'Don't worry,' she said. 'You have a nice body, we can easily cover that up with make-up if it doesn't fade.'

They let me put my clothes back on and I felt much better. It was as if I had passed a test; faced my fears and conquered them. They were being so nice to me I felt foolish for making such a fuss. They must have thought I was a silly, innocent girl from the country.

'Would you like to go for a rehearsal now?' the Australian lady asked.

'What's a rehearsal?' I asked.

'They'll teach you how to dance.'

'Okay,' I said.

It was as if I'd passed a milestone in my life and moved on. I'd overcome my inhibitions by taking my clothes off in front of them and now they were offering me a chance to do something different, something that would allow me to fulfil my dream of helping my family. I felt proud.

For three weeks I was rehearsing and practising the dances. Life was suddenly a whirl of new experiences and new faces, distracting me from the feelings of anxiety and homesickness that still took over when I was lying in bed waiting for sleep, listening to the night noises of strangers, or whenever I had a moment to myself. To begin with I felt very shy; seeing the other girls walking around naked in the changing rooms made me want to panic and run home, but I knew I couldn't. Until I'd earned some money I didn't even have enough for the bus ticket. Sometimes when the other girls put make-up on my face and I saw the transformation in the mirror, my courage would return and I would relax for a while, feeling part of the group. People kept telling me how beautiful I was, trying to make me more comfortable, and that was nice. There was always so much noise and chatter and laughter. We could often laugh together and have fun, but I didn't feel I could ever be close to them. Something about the way they talked and behaved made me feel I couldn't trust any of them. I kept losing things like make-up, shoes and — later on — cash. I had no idea who might be taking them so I never said anything. I didn't want to get a reputation for being a troublemaker.

There were about ten of us 'show dancers' and about 50 more regular dancers, who performed for the customers between our shows while we had a break, talked to customers or got changed. There were around five shows a night, lasting about half an hour each. We started by performing some slow ballads, with seductive movements, wearing either two-piece outfits or mini skirts and tight blouses with black tights and ballet shoes. After about three songs we changed into bikinis and Madonna-style pointy, sequinned bras, and then into a variety of dresses. It felt good to be wearing glamorous clothes and I liked seeing myself all made-up and ready to go on stage. It surprised me to see how grown-up I looked, and how different to the little girl who had worked almost invisibly in her auntie's house for so long. It made me proud to think I was now an independent woman, but at the same time there was always a feeling of loneliness and sadness in the background that I couldn't quite shake off.

I didn't have to be naked after all, which was a relief, and once I'd learned the dances I really enjoyed performing. I made sure I got on well with the other girls, avoiding the arguments that sometimes broke out between them. Usually they were arguing about men. It was a bit like having a new family, but one that knew nothing of my past or my problems, and one that I didn't think I would ever grow to love. I was just one of them and that was a nice feeling. None of us ever talked about our pasts or how we had come to be at the club. It was as if we all wanted to keep a little distance.

As well as the dancers there were also the receptionists who entertained the customers at their tables and bought them drinks, but didn't dance.

Each night a make-up artist would come in and we would pay him to give us different looks, like children play-acting at being something we weren't.

Several of the girls who watched the show told me I was the best one in it, which made me happy. It felt so nice to be appreciated and praised for something I was doing. The customers I got to meet were all very complimentary and friendly as well. The house rules said no one was allowed to touch us in the club and the men all respected that.

I was being paid the equivalent of about £30 a day just to dance. If a customer bought me a drink between shows I would be given half the cost of the drink, which could double the amount of money I earned. Sometimes a customer would tip me as well. Suddenly I was rich beyond anything I'd ever imagined possible. The other girls would often ask to borrow money and I was always pleased to lend it, even though I soon learned I would seldom get it back. I don't think any of them ever needed the money; they were just in the habit of scrounging it from anyone they thought would be a soft touch. Sometimes I thought they didn't even know they were doing it.

Because I was more than happy with what I was being paid, I didn't feel I had to fight and hustle for more, which is how some of the other girls behaved. I think the customers could tell I was content just to be friendly and that I wasn't always going to be looking for ways to get them to spend more. They responded to me well, telling me I was different to the others. I never asked them for money but they always gave me more than the other girls. I got a reputation in the club for being lucky. I got as many compliments about my personality as I did about my looks and my dancing, even though I spoke virtually no English at all. It felt wonderful to believe that people actually liked me and I looked forward to going in to work every day.

Although I was earning a lot of money there were some expenses as well. Three times a week we all had to go to a clinic for a smear test, to check we were clean of sexually transmitted diseases. We would be given yellow cards in order to work, which we then had to show every time we came into the club. Not only did we have to pay for the tests, but I had to pay for taxis every time because I knew that if I went in a jeepney I'd get lost in the maze of city backstreets. At heart I was still a little country girl, trying to find my way in the big city.

When I was first told we had to go to the doctors, I couldn't understand why. I asked one of the other girls what it was all about.

'It's in case you go out with one of the customers,' she explained. 'They need to know you're clean and are not carrying disease. Everyone's frightened about AIDS. If you have an infection the doctors will give you antibiotics and you'll have to stay off work until it clears up. They give us pink cards until we're cleared; then they give us the yellow cards again.'

'Go out with one of the customers?' I asked, trying to understand what she was telling me.

'They can buy you out,' she explained wearily, obviously surprised by my ignorance. 'If you agree to go with them they pay a bar fine, which you get a share of, and then you can keep anything they give you outside the bar. A pretty girl like you could make a lot of money if you wanted to.'

'Oh,' I said, 'I see.'

By that time I knew the club and the people there and I knew no one would make me do anything I didn't want to, so I wasn't frightened by the revelations, more intrigued really. Some of the girls didn't seem to mind who they went with. Some would even let the doctors at the clinic have sex with them in the cubicles rather than pay for their smear tests. Many of them were very beautiful and I could understand why the doctors might be tempted.

I wondered if I would ever meet a customer I liked enough to agree to go out with them.

CHAPTER SEVEN

Lonely Hotel Rooms

The first customer to take me out of the bar was an Egyptian man. By then I was 19 years old. I'd talked to lots of customers at the tables, even though it was usually impossible to communicate beyond smiles, nods and simple sign language. I only had a few words of English, which I was picking up from the customers and the other girls as I went along, but some of the men had none at all. They came from as far afield as Japan and Germany and their accents were so different even the English words they did know were incomprehensible to my ears. I just kept smiling and laughing, trying to put them at their ease and make them believe I was enjoying their company. In many cases I was.

I'd been asked out by quite a few of them but I was nervous about being taken away from the bar because I still didn't know the city well. I was frightened that if they took me to a part of Manila I didn't recognise, I'd never find my way back to the club or to the house where I was staying with the other girls, or to Beth and Josie's new house, which I'd still only visited once at that stage.

I was also afraid customers might take me to places that were posher than anything I had experienced before and I wouldn't know what to do or how to behave. I could tell from the clothes the men wore, their watches and the way they spent money on us, that they came from a different world to anything I was used to. I was wary about stepping into such an unknown place. Would people stare at me? Would they let me in or, if they did, would they ask me to leave once it became obvious I was a bar girl? What would I ask for to eat or drink? Which knife and fork should I use? What would I talk about?

The Egyptian was in his thirties, and not bad looking. He'd come into the club alone and sat watching the show intently, applauding enthusiastically after each number. At the end he asked the Mama San, the woman who was in charge of all the girls, if he could meet me. That was how it was done; they weren't supposed to talk to us directly until we had been introduced.

I went across to his table and he stood up politely, offering to buy me a drink. Normally I would have asked for a coke because we had to make sure we stayed sober enough to be able to do the next show. This time, however, I felt a little bold and asked for a Margarita, a name I'd heard the other girls using. I had no idea what it would taste like but when I sipped it I liked it. After a few more sips it seemed to make my self-consciousness fade slightly, but I had to be careful the boss didn't see me drinking alcohol so early in the evening. I began to feel a little daring, like a naughty schoolgirl defying school rules.

'Will you come out with me?' the Egyptian asked after a few minutes of small talk and I felt a flutter of nerves in my stomach despite the Margarita.

He was the nicest man I'd talked to in the club so far, with very good manners and impeccable English, but I was still frightened of where he would take me, how I would cope with all the people and how I would get back afterwards. Emboldened by the Margarita I took a deep breath.

'Okay,' I said.

He called the Mama San over and paid the required bar fine while I waited, smiling hard to cover my nerves. Outside the club he hailed a taxi and we climbed in. Within seconds of the driver setting off I was lost and disorientated. I peered anxiously out of the window, trying to memorise the route, but none of the buildings looked familiar and I lost track of how many times we turned left or right. Soon everything we passed looked much bigger and smarter and cleaner than I was used to. We were obviously in a better area and I had no idea how I would get back from here. I said nothing, just kept smiling.

The taxi dropped us outside the grand front doors of a five-star hotel and my date escorted me in, past smiling doormen in smart uniforms and across a wide, shiny marble floor, beneath chandeliers and past a long reception desk staffed by a line of immaculately groomed people. There were giant flower arrangements and soft music. Luxurious sofas and chairs, like I'd only ever seen in magazines, were grouped together for guests to sit and talk. It was as if I'd crossed the threshold into a different world. It smelled of perfume. I was glad I was dressed and made-up discreetly and didn't look as if I'd been working in a bar. I wouldn't have wanted to draw any of these eyes towards me.

The Egyptian strode confidently across to the restaurant and I almost had to run to keep up with him. He spoke quietly to the headwaiter who bowed his head respectfully and led us to a table in a discreet corner, spread napkins across our laps and gave us enormous menus which I could make no sense of at all. The table was laid up with rows of glasses and cutlery gleaming in the dim lighting.

My new friend must have realised I had no idea what to do or what to ask for and he ordered for me with only the briefest of glances in my direction to check I wasn't protesting. I kept smiling and nodding and hoping for the best. The glasses were filled with wine and water, and delicious food was laid in front of me. I watched my host carefully and followed whatever he did. We tried to make conversation but it was very difficult now that we had exhausted all the usual superficial chitchat. This wasn't the time or place to start asking each other deep, personal questions, not that I would have known where to start. I wasn't at all sure if Egypt was a country or a city and I certainly didn't have a clue where in the world it was. So most of the time I was just looking round the beautiful room at all the other people, feeling like I was dreaming.

When we'd finished the meal we strolled up to his bedroom. It was huge – a sitting room and bedroom all in one, but bigger than any house I'd ever lived in. Even the bed was larger than life and when I tried sitting in one of the armchairs my feet didn't touch the floor. I walked around with my mouth open like a tourist, examining the cut glass decanters on the bar, the pictures on the wall, the glossy magazines beside the bed.

'Help yourself to anything you want,' he said.

'No, it's okay,' I replied, continuing to explore and stare.

The bathroom was like a palace, filled with fluffy white towels and I felt so proud of myself for having plucked up the courage to come to such a place. I tried out everything, coming back into the bedroom smelling of a variety of soaps and sprays.

He was sweet and gentle but when he touched me it made me think of Jun. The sadness welled up inside me because I still only wanted to be touching my husband, no one else. He saw I was crying and stepped back, passing me a tissue.

'We don't have to do anything, you know,' he said. 'We can just go to sleep. Don't be frightened.'

He seemed a very nice man and I believed he meant what he said. I felt bad for disappointing him but grateful to him for being so understanding of my fears.

'It's okay,' I assured him and climbed into the huge bed.

The sheets were crisp and scented and I kept crying because I felt dirty just from being there. He cuddled me and comforted me and slowly I relaxed my inhibitions in the cool, dimly lit room, allowing him to caress and kiss me until, eventually, he was no longer comforting me like a brother and we were having sex. He was kind and considerate and didn't hurt me, but I received no pleasure from anything that happened between us because in my mind I wanted to be somewhere else, with someone else.

'How long have you been working in the bar?' he asked when it was all over and we were lying next to each other on the deep soft pillows.

'About a month.'

'How many customers have you been out with?'

'You're the first.'

'No!' He looked genuinely surprised. 'But with your looks there must have been many men asking.'

'Yes,' I said, 'but you were the first one I said yes to.'

It must have sounded like the sort of line every bar girl would say, believing it would be what the man would want to hear. But he didn't seem to doubt my word. After a while he stopped asking questions and I realised he'd fallen asleep. As I lay on my back, staring at the ceiling, listening to his peaceful breathing beside me, I imagined how much more Jun would hate me now after what I'd just done. How could I ever hope that he and I might get back together to make a family for Dailyn now? I'd crossed a bridge into a different world and I would never be able to go back. As the hours drifted slowly past I started to worry about what I would do in the morning and how I would find my way back to the club or my house. The more I worried the more awake I became, waiting to see the inevitable arrival of dawn through the cracks in the curtains.

When he woke the Egyptian asked if I would like some breakfast.

'Okay,' I said, not really knowing what I wanted, and he ordered some things over the phone.

About 20 minutes later a waiter knocked on the door and wheeled in a trolley filled with plates, glasses, jugs of juice, fruit and silver tea and coffee pots. The plates were covered with silver domes to keep the food warm. When the domes were lifted by their ornate handles, I just laughed to see so much food for two people.

'I'll never eat all this,' I protested.

'It's okay,' he said. 'Just eat what you want.'

As we ate we talked some more.

'You're a nice girl,' he said after a while.

'Thank you.' I liked him too.

When I'd eaten all the breakfast I could manage and had stood for ages under the warm powerful shower in the bathroom, trying to wash away my guilty conscience, he asked, 'Where are you going now?'

His question reminded me I didn't know where I was and I felt the panic rising again. I couldn't even remember the name of the club where I worked.

'I don't know where I'm going,' I confessed. 'I've forgotten the name of the club. Do you remember it?'

'No,' he admitted, 'I didn't notice the name. What about your home?'

'It's a long way away,' I said. 'I've always gone there on the bus from the club but I can't remember where it is. I know the name of the area where my sister lives, but not exactly where the house is.'

He thought for a moment, obviously worried on my behalf.

'I'll tell you what,' he said, taking out his wallet and counting out about US$50, 'I'll get you a taxi.' He'd already given me my money for the night.

I began to feel better. With enough money for a taxi I felt sure I could eventually locate Beth's house. I'd been to see it just a few days before I met the Egyptian. Beth had been the only one there because Josie had gone back to the mountains to fetch the children so they could all live together, and she had invited me to move in with them too. The idea of being with Beth again made me very happy. The month or so I'd spent living in the house with the other girls had helped me to become more independent and to make new friends. I knew now that I could survive on my own if I had to, but I still liked the idea of being part of a family again, my family. I would have my own home to go to in Manila for the first time.

The Egyptian found me a sympathetic taxi driver outside the hotel and we said goodbye a little awkwardly, not sure whether to act like friends or just business acquaintances. I told the taxi driver the name of the area where Beth's house was, hoping that once I got there I would be able to recognise the street. As I watched his eyes in the mirror I was horribly aware he must know exactly what had happened between me and the Egyptian, but he gave no indication if he did. I guess he saw girls like me coming out of hotels in the morning all the time.

He took me to the marketplace in the area I wanted and dropped me off. Although I was worried about how to find the house I wasn't able to resist the stalls and started spending the Egyptian's money on clothes and food. I'd never had so much cash in my purse at any one time and it felt wonderful. As I went from stall to stall, asking to be shown things and haggling over prices, I was able to forget how I'd earned the money. It took me back to my childhood in the markets of Sorsogon, when we were always trying to sell and it was other people who had the money to buy the pretty things. I wanted to surprise Beth and Josie and the kids by walking through the door with piles of presents. I couldn't wait to see the delight on their faces. It would be like Christmas.

Once I was loaded down with as many parcels and plastic bags as I could carry, I knew it was time to start searching seriously for the house. I waved down one of the motorised tricycles that carry people around in their sidecars.

'Where are you going Ma'am?' the driver asked as I piled my parcels into the sidecar.

'I don't know exactly,' I admitted. 'It's somewhere around here but I can't remember which street. It's a cul-de-sac. If you drive around for a while maybe I'll be able to recognise it.'

'That's going to be hard,' he sighed, but smiled anyway as I clambered in and settled myself amongst the shopping. We set off, cruising up and down every street as I peered around, trying to spot something familiar. We must have been searching in vain for about four hours and I was starting to feel deeply self-conscious.

'Don't worry,' I said. 'Whatever it costs I'll pay.'

'That's okay,' he assured me, 'as long as I can get you home.'

As the light began to fade my hopes faded with it, and I wondered what I would do if I never found the right road. I could imagine Beth and her reunited family sitting down to tea, all happy and cosy in their home, while I was forced to roam the streets on my own forever.

'It has to be the next one,' the driver said eventually, 'because we've tried every other street in the area.'

'It's here!' I shouted as we turned the last corner and I recognised it. 'This is it!'

I was so grateful to him for being so helpful I paid him double what he asked for and ran into the house clutching all the packages. Beth and the children were jumping around with excitement when they saw what I'd brought them. Everyone was so happy.

'Where did you get so much money?' Beth asked later as the children were tucking into the food and Josie had gone out to meet some friends.

'I went out with a customer from the club,' I said, avoiding her eyes.

'Oh, Gina,' she said, her pretty, dark little face suddenly grave. 'Promise me you'll be very, very careful.'

'I promise,' I said and she gave me a hug. Not knowing what else to say we both started laughing and turned our attention back to the children. Now that I was back amongst friends and family I knew I would be able to work out how to find the club again the next day.

When I was alone again in bed that night, I thought about what I'd done with the Egyptian. It had been so easy. All the stories and warnings I'd heard from the nurses at the hospital about girls becoming sick with AIDS and other diseases haunted the back of my mind, making me feel sick with apprehension. What if I had already been infected? We had used a condom, but I knew they didn't protect you from everything. I knew that having sex with strangers was dangerous, but it felt good to have so much money in my purse and to know I would have more than enough to send back to my parents this month. It wouldn't be long before I would be able to start building them the stone house I'd dreamed of for so long. I had also been given a glimpse into a different world, a place where people always had the money for whatever they needed, where food was available whenever you were hungry and you didn't have to work every hour of the day because other people would do all the chores for you. In the world of the wealthy you didn't have to fear typhoons as you lay in your bed, the chances were you wouldn't even hear them through the thick stone walls and double glazing. That was a world I wanted my family to inhabit.

Having done it once and come to no harm, it was much easier to accept the next time a customer invited me out of the club. Sometimes they'd ask me out and not want to have sex; they would just want someone to go with them for a meal or dancing, someone for company in a city a long way from home. The warm tropical evenings must be hard for men who want to stay faithful to their wives and partners. During the day they're distracted by their jobs but at night they're alone, either in their hotel rooms staring at the television or drinking in bars. It's not surprising they want someone to talk to for a few hours now and again.

If they suggested leaving the club I would always ask where we would be going before I agreed, still nervous about being taken to an area I didn't know and being unable to find my way back. I was lucky because none of the men I went out with ever treated me badly, and they were always generous with money. They came from all over the world. There was even a famous Filipino actor in the club one evening. All the girls were trying to persuade him to dance with them, but he grabbed me and I felt so proud as we whirled around the dance floor together. It was unusual to actually be able to speak the same language as a customer.

When I was enjoying myself and having fun with the other girls and with the customers, I was able to forget sometimes that this wasn't the place I wanted to be, particularly if I had had a few drinks. Where I wanted to be most of all was in a little house somewhere by the sea with Jun and Dailyn. But if that wasn't possible, I reasoned, it was better to have fun and meet new people than to sit around being miserable. The occasional drink would help to suppress the sadness whenever it threatened to rise up again.

One night a group of American men came into the club, all dressed up in women's clothes and wearing make-up. One of them was so pretty he could have been a girl, even though his hair was shaved close to his scalp. He was so tiny and so sweet. He kept smiling at me while I was dancing and beckoning me over to have a drink. Intrigued, I went over and asked for a coke. We talked for a bit and he asked if he could take me out of the club. I laughed, thinking he was joking because I couldn't imagine he would be interested in me.

'No,' he said, his face serious, 'I mean it.'

I felt so comfortable with him I was very happy to accept the invitation and see what happened.

'Where are you staying?' I asked, wondering as usual how I would get back.

'I live on a ship,' he said. 'We're in the American Navy. Would you like to see the ship?'

'Okay,' I laughed.

'I'll have to smuggle you on, we're not allowed visitors on board.'

The guards must have been distracted somewhere else because we managed to get on board without anybody challenging us. The security was very relaxed and there hardly seemed to be anyone around. He led me below decks, through a maze of corridors all looking the same, to his cabin. Once we were safely inside he showed me all the dresses and women's clothes he kept in his locker.

'Are you a girl or a boy?' I was confused but I was so comfortable I felt I could ask him anything.

'I'm a boy,' he laughed. 'So, if you didn't know which I was, why did you come with me?'

'Because you're so sweet,' I teased. 'Are we going to have sex or what?'

'You're joking, aren't you? I only invited you out because I liked you. I don't do sex.'

'Okay,' I said, feeling partly relieved and partly disappointed.

We stayed in the cabin until late, having something to eat, talking and tickling one another. It was like being with one of my girlfriends, so easy and comfortable. I just wanted to squeeze his little face like a particularly cute child.

'I have to take you back now,' he said eventually and we left the ship, with him still in his dress, and again no one stopped us. Not wanting the night to end we stopped at another club for a drink on the way and he delivered me back to Jools just before dawn. The next day he came to look for me again, this time in his military uniform. He asked if I would come out with him again.

'What for?' I wanted to know.

'I just like your company,' he shrugged, as if puzzled by my puzzlement.

That night we went all over Manila, dancing and drinking. He kissed me on the lips a few times, but that was all. It was really nice to know him.

Another customer was a Canadian who was so handsome all the girls wanted him to pick them. He'd been going out a few times with one of the other girls and she wasn't pleased when he picked me instead. At that time my skin had reacted badly to the make-up I wore each night and had come out with a rash of spots.

'Look at your poor face,' he said when he saw me in the light. 'What a shame. I'm going to Canada for a couple of days, I'll try to get you something.'

I was very touched that he cared enough to do that, even though he didn't know me. He took me out twice but we never had sex. He brought me the cream as he promised, but the girl he'd been going out with before became so jealous I didn't want to go any further with him. She kept calling me names and threatening to punch me. I didn't put up any sort of fight, just promised not to see him again. It didn't seem worth creating a bad atmosphere amongst the girls over a customer, even one as good-looking as him. I knew how she felt because I experienced the same pangs when I saw him talking to another girl, but I didn't say anything. Next time he asked me out I said no.

'Why not?' he asked, obviously surprised.

'Because you have a girlfriend,' I nodded towards the girl.

'She's not my girlfriend,' he said. 'I just talk to her, like I talk to you.'

'Have you had sex with her?'

'Yeah. But it was a long time ago. Come out with me, please.'

I was surprised how much it hurt me to think of him with someone else and I agreed to go out one more time, even though I'd said I wouldn't. When we got to his hotel room he was talking about a bad car accident he'd had, when he was nearly killed. He had a metal plate in his back, and since then he hadn't been able to have sex.

'I just like to go out with girls for company.'

He asked me to tell him what I was doing at the club. 'You seem too nice to be doing that sort of work.'

I explained how I was trying to earn enough money to build a stone house for my family. I spent the night with him and the next morning, after breakfast, he gave me some money to send home. All the customers I met were kind to me like that, and I was surprised by how often they didn't want full sex. There was one who just liked to feel girls' boobs; he was a bit disappointed with me because he wanted to be able to get a good handful. I was always relieved if I didn't have to do anything which might give me a disease. The one time I caught anything it was only a urine infection and it cleared up quickly. Only one customer ever refused to use a condom, which worried me a lot. But when I went to the doctors for my next check up I was clear.

I was normally good at judging which men would be gentle and kind and I only ever made one bad mistake. He was a European man with a badly scarred face, which added to his air of menace. The moment we got to his hotel he wanted sex, jumping on me with all his clothes still on. There was something wrong and I felt frightened.

'I can't wait to make love to you,' he said.

'Hang on a moment,' I said, 'why don't we have a wash first?'

'Okay,' he agreed, 'that's a good idea.'

'You go first.'

As soon as he was safely in the bathroom I made a run for it and returned to the club. A few minutes later he turned up again and went straight to the Mama San.

'I asked you to choose me a good girl,' he told her, 'and you said that one wouldn't let me down. But she ran away from me.'

The Mama San came over to where I was sitting, trying to pretend I hadn't noticed he was back.

'Why did you run away from him?' she asked.

'Mama San, he scared me to death,' I told her.

She patted my hand understandingly and went back to make some excuse on my behalf. Maybe he wasn't such a bad man because he still gave her some money to pass on to me.

Another customer offered to pay me whatever I wanted for sex, but when he started kissing me I couldn't stand the smell of his breath. He was sad when I said I wasn't going to stay, but he didn't try to stop me.

One evening a very rich Chinese man took me back to his hotel. Only when I lay down on the bed did I notice there was a mirror on the ceiling. I was still fully clothed when he jumped on me, having stripped off his own clothes with lightning speed. The sight of the back of his bald head in the mirror as he set about kissing me was too much for me, making me want to laugh, and I had to tell him I couldn't go through with it. He was really cross with me and didn't pay me anything, but it was always more important to me that I felt comfortable with what I was doing than that I was paid.

One evening a Filipino girl came into the club with her husband, who was Japanese. They had another Japanese man with them who looked very elderly.

The girl asked the Mama San to recommend a nice girl who they could trust to spend time with their friend and the Mama San pointed to me. They called me over and talked for a while before the girl asked if I would be willing to provide their elderly friend with some company.

'Don't worry, he wouldn't dream of asking for sex,' the girl assured me, as if reading my mind. 'He's 81 years old. He just wants someone to go with him to the islands for a holiday.'

'Okay,' I said. 'I'll go with him to the islands and look after him. That would be nice, if it's okay with him.'

'Oh yes,' she said. 'He likes you.'

The old man and I travelled to the beach resort and, although we shared a room, there was no sex. He did joke with me that he had some Viagra if I wanted him to use it, but I told him to forget it. We talked a lot and laughed. He told me about his family in Japan, and about how he had been on his own for many years. I would talk about my family in the mountains. I never told my customers about what happened to Jun. I didn't want to frighten them. I could see why the Filipina and her husband had been looking for a girl they could trust because the old man was very relaxed about everything, often leaving piles of money lying around the room. He bought me some clothes and we had some nice meals together. It was a very pleasant holiday.

'What do you want from your life?' he asked over dinner one evening.

'I just want to help my family,' I replied.

'Why do you do this sort of work?'

'Because I thought it would be an easy way to make some money,' I said. 'I have no education for anything else.'

'I feel sorry for you,' he said. 'You're a nice girl. What would you like me to give you as a souvenir of this holiday?'

I thought for a minute. 'I've always wanted a radio.'

'I have a radio in the hotel in Manila. I'll give it to you. It's a very expensive one.'

'That's very kind, thank you.'

When we got back to the city he gave me the radio. It was beautiful, small and heavy. It was possible to play tapes on it as well. I was thrilled.

'What else do you want?' he asked.

'Nothing else,' I said, stroking my new toy lovingly. 'I will look after this.'

He gave me a gold necklace as well, which I lost later, but I still have the radio today. He had also given me the equivalent of about £600 in cash during the four days, so I was now able to send my dad enough money to start work on the stone house.

The house I'd been sharing with Beth and her family had a problem with flooding. Whenever there was a heavy rainfall the water would run into the cellar and the smell of damp became unbearable, so we moved to a new place. Sometimes, of course, I would disappear for a day or two with a customer and Beth wouldn't know when I was coming back, but most of the time I was just part of the family and I was able to forget the world of the club.

When I did come back after a few days away it was always like a party, my purse usually being full of money. I would go shopping and fill the house with food and drink, giving them whatever they wanted. Josie's mother would do all my washing and laundry for me and I would pay her well. If neighbours dropped in during one of our celebrations they would wonder what the occasion was, but it was just an ordinary day for us because we wanted to enjoy our good luck while it lasted.

One day, while I was away, Beth had taken the children to stay with her mother-in-law and when I got home I found the house had been ransacked by thieves. I had a collection of miniature drinks bottles from minibars in hotels I'd visited and they'd all been drunk and left strewn around. I'd been keeping about £3,000 in cash in the house as well, waiting to pay the builders in

Bintan-o, but that too had gone. I felt like I'd lost everything after all I'd had to do to earn it. I was suspicious of the neighbours and decided we should move again to a nicer, more secure area. The robbery spurred me on to try even harder to improve my life, so I could earn more to finish my parents' house before my luck ran out.

Whenever I made a trip home to the mountains I took groceries and gifts for everyone, including clothes and ornaments. We were all so pleased to see one another again and everyone was excited by the things I'd brought with me. Some of my dad's relations said I should have brought more, but I did all I could. Mum and Dad were always very grateful for whatever I gave them. I think they knew I was trying my hardest to keep my word and repay them for all the trouble I'd caused.

'How are you earning all this money?' Dad asked one evening the first time I went back, when no one else was listening.

'I'm working in a club, Papa,' I said. When I looked up, I could see he was crying.

'Why do you have to do that?' he asked.

'I told you in the letter when I left,' I said, unable to stop my own tears. 'I will do whatever is necessary to pay you back.'

CHAPTER EIGHT

New York, New York

The next customer I went out with was an American. He was in his thirties and a little bit chubby. He'd been sitting in the club for a while before I was called to his table, but I'd been ignoring him. I never liked to give customers the impression I was hustling for company. I only wanted men to ask for me if they really liked the look of me, not because I appeared desperate. Maybe that was why they were always so nice to me.

I'd noticed a lot of the girls were making a big fuss of him but I had no idea why and I didn't intend to start competing for his attention. When the Mama San told me he wanted to meet me, however, I was quite happy to go. Like most Americans he was very open and polite, which made him easy to talk to. He told me how nice I was, which I was growing used to hearing but was still pleasant. He also told me his name was Bill.

'Would you like to go out with me?' he asked after we'd been talking for a while.

'Okay,' I said, but he didn't immediately get up to pay the bar fine and go, which is what usually happened. I took my cue from him and waited to see what he wanted to do next.

One of the ordinary dancers was sent to the table by the Mama San and Bill asked her the same question. She agreed as well. I wondered if I'd made a mistake, or if I'd misunderstood, or given him the impression I didn't want to go out with him. I was confused so I stayed quiet and watched. I'd never been in a situation like this before and I was worried about what would happen next. If he was planning to take more than one of us out, what would be expected of me? I could have changed my mind at that stage but he seemed a good-natured man and I didn't want to hurt his feelings or make a fuss, so I decided to go along with whatever he was planning. The other girl didn't seem at all bothered about me being there as well.

He took us back to the hotel, where they had a disco, and then to the restaurant for something to eat. Once we'd eaten we went up to his room, not having any idea what he had planned.

'Just help yourselves to whatever you want,' he said, gesturing around the room.

It was a nice room, much like all the ones I'd been to with other customers. Having become more confident in such surroundings with experience, I went into the bath-room and decided to have a hot bath. I wasn't in any hurry to do anything else and it seemed a pity to waste the opportunity for a bit of pampering. The tub filled quickly and I used the hotel bubble bath, making it froth up to the edges. I undressed and lowered myself through the cold bubbles into the hot, fragrant water. The American and the other girl were coming and going, but I wasn't taking much notice, just enjoying the luxury of the moment.

As I lay in the bubbles an unusual smell drifted through from the other room, which didn't seem like normal cigarettes to me. Once I'd soaked for long enough, I climbed out, dried and wrapped myself in one of the fluffy hotel robes, going through to the bedroom to see what was happening.

'Anyone want the bath?' I asked and they both disap-peared into the bathroom while I dried my hair at the dressing table mirror.

The strange, sweet aroma hung in the air and I could tell they were smoking something in the bathroom. I still wasn't quite sure what was happening because I'd never come across someone hiring more than one girl at a time before, although I'd heard of it. I finished drying my hair.

When they emerged from the bathroom they were very wrapped up in one another and started having sex on the bed in front of me. I didn't say anything but I averted my eyes, embarrassed, not sure what I was expected to do.

'Do you want to lie down with us?' Bill asked.

'No,' I said.

I didn't like the idea of having him pulling his penis out of her and sticking it straight into me. It seemed like the riskiest thing to do and I didn't want to catch anything and have to be off work for a week or more. I'd had enough warnings from the nurses at the clinic to know how great the risks were with this sort of thing. I was also on my period at the time, which would have made it embarrassing. I waited until they'd finished and he was lying on the bed, panting and exhausted, and then, not wanting him to think he wasn't getting his money's worth, I gave him a massage. He accepted my attentions without a word, sighing with pleasure as he relaxed beneath my fingers. After a while he sat up, pressed some money into the other girl's hand and sent her home.

'What about me?' I asked.

'No,' he said, 'you can stay here.'

I didn't feel worried about being on my own with him by that time. He seemed a very gentle, kind man. Once the other girl had gone I lay down on the bed beside him and we talked. My English, too, was becoming more confident with experience. He told me he lived in New York and that he'd never been married.

'I really like you,' he said. 'It's great to have someone to talk to. You're very different to the other girls. You seem too sweet for this sort of work.'

'Oh,' I said, 'that's very kind of you to say so.'

Most of my early photos
were swept away in
Typhoon Sisang, but this
is of me going for a wash
in Panlayaan, aged 18.

My brother, Christopher,
with the family carabaw.

My daughter, Dailyn.

When living with Bill in New York.

He asked me about my life and my family and I told him about Dailyn and that I was working to send money for her and for my parents.

I stayed the whole night, but he didn't suggest we had sex. When we woke up in the morning he showed me a collection of perfumes he had in the room, all of them in enormous bottles.

'When you go home,' he said, 'choose one of these to take with you.'

'I don't know which one to choose,' I said, never having owned a bottle of really expensive perfume in my life.

'My favourite is Opium,' he said.

'Okay,' I said, 'I'll take that one. Thank you.'

'That's class,' he said, 'you'll like that. It'll last you a long time.'

When I got home I read the bottle and saw the words 'toilet water'. I assumed that it must be for freshening the toilet and bathroom after use, which seemed quite a good idea to me. Every time I came into the house after that I wandered around, spraying it everywhere. I'd used the whole bottle in a few weeks!

'It's been good getting to know you,' he said when I was leaving. 'I'd like to meet you again.'

'Would you really?' I said, genuinely surprised, since I'd imagined he would be looking for more girls who liked to smoke pot and have sex with him.

★

I loved having money to indulge Beth and her family. It made me feel I was valuable to them. Sometimes we'd go into a department store and I'd tell them to pick whatever they wanted. They'd choose things they'd never had before in their lives, luxury items they could never have afforded for themselves. If one of them had a birthday I would arrange a party, and I made sure I paid for the house and the furniture. It made me feel good to know I wasn't useless and lazy as my parents had told me so often.

Working such late hours was always exhausting and sometimes I would doze off on the late bus home. One night I fell so soundly asleep I missed my stop and my head lolled onto the shoulder of the man sitting next to me. When I woke up he was stroking me very gently, like you would a child.

'Oh, I'm sorry,' I stuttered, feeling foolish and embarrassed. 'I'm just so tired. I've come from work.'

'Where do you work?' he asked.

'The Holiday Inn.' I said the first thing that came into my head. 'On the reception desk.'

'Where do you live?' he asked and I told him, just making conversation.

A few days later there was a knock on our front door and the man from the bus was standing on the doorstep.

'I was thinking about you,' he said, 'so I thought I'd pop in and say hello.'

I was so shocked to see him I couldn't think what to say, so I invited him in.

'I went to the Holiday Inn to look for you,' he said once he was sitting down, drinking coffee.

'Oh,' I said, immediately feeling guilty. 'I'm sorry. I lied about where I work. I was a bit embarrassed and I didn't want you to know I worked in a bar.'

'You don't have to work in a bar,' he said, looking sad.

'It's for my family.' I shrugged.

'Well, if it's what you want …'

'It's not what I want. It's just the only way to make enough money. You don't want to know a girl like me.'

'Why not?' He seemed surprised. 'Lots of girls have to do that sort of work, and most of them don't have your personality. You're a decent woman.'

'No,' I shook my head. 'I don't want to see you.'

He was a nice man, but he wasn't my type. I still loved Jun in my heart and, although I'd learned to keep what I did with the customers in a separate compartment of my mind, I didn't feel ready to replace him with someone else in my heart. My emotions were a mess, my heart yearning to be back with my husband and child, even though being with customers was not as bad as I'd imagined it would be.

A few days after he'd first taken me out, Bill the American came back to the club and asked for me. We went out for a meal and then back to his hotel room. It was good to see him, like meeting up with an old friend, but I wasn't sure what he was hoping would happen this time.

'I'd like to take you somewhere,' he said after we'd been talking for some time.

'Where?' I asked, only half listening.

'New York.'

The name meant nothing to me. It was just another city. I assumed it was in America but I had no idea whether it was near or far. I'd often heard people talking about the foreign countries they'd been to and the adventures they'd had, but I had no idea where these places were or what they looked like. When people tried to explain different time zones to me it made my head ache, I just couldn't see how it was possible that it could be different times in different places at the same moment. My only experience of America was the news programmes I saw flickering past on the television screens in the hotel rooms I visited, and I'd never really understood what they were talking about or the context of anything they said or any of the pictures they showed.

If it had been the handsome Canadian man who was asking me to go travelling with him I would have been surer about how I felt. I could even have imagined myself falling for him. The same would have been true with the sweet little American soldier in the women's clothes. But I couldn't imagine myself falling for Bill, and it didn't seem fair to let him take me to America if I didn't fancy him. I liked him as a friend and felt comfortable with him, but was that enough to risk getting on an airplane and going to a strange country?

Just a few months before I'd been frightened about travelling to different parts of Manila for fear I might not be able to find my way home, frightened even of leaving my sister's side, and now I was being invited to a foreign city. How would I ever find my way back from there? At the same time I now knew I could survive in the world on my own. My confidence had grown and this man was offering me an opportunity for an adventure that might never come my way again. I might not know anything about New York, but I could tell it would be something new and exciting. It would be as big an adventure as my first trip to Manila had been, all those years before.

'You don't have to be frightened,' he said, 'I'll look after you.'

'I know,' I said. But it wasn't that easy to trust some-one who was virtually a stranger.

'Get yourself a passport anyway,' he suggested and I thought there was no harm in that. I could always change my mind later.

My mind changed back and forth a hundred times in the coming weeks as I waited for my passport to arrive. One moment I would be excited at the prospect of a holiday in America, and then I would become frightened of what might go wrong and how far from home I would be. Eventually the passport came and I ran out of excuses not to take the risk. I didn't know how long exactly he was inviting me to New York for, but I assumed I would be safely back in Manila in a week or

two. It would be silly to pass up such an opportunity. Bill
still hadn't asked for sex and assured me he just wanted
to spend time with me. I was beginning to trust him.

I told the Mama San I was going away for a week or
so, but promised I would be back and she wished me
luck. I put on the smart suit Bill had bought me for travelling, packed a few extra clothes in a bag and went to
meet him at his hotel. It was all so easy and so smooth.
A taxi delivered us to the airport, a place Bill went
through all the time, and we were shown to an executive
lounge because we were travelling business class. I'd
never been to an airport before, let alone business class,
with all the free food and drink and being treated like a
VIP. I'd had no idea what to expect, but I certainly
hadn't expected anything like this from the stories I'd
heard told by other travelling Filipinas. I wished I could
eat some of the elegant little snacks they were offering
but my heart was pounding so fast from a mixture of
nerves and excitement that it was hard to breathe, let
alone chew and swallow.

The inside of the plane was as luxurious as the
lounge, with wide seats and more legroom than a little
person like me could ever need. Bill was completely
relaxed and did his best to make me feel the same. As
children my brothers and I had often stared up at the
planes flying over the islands and wondered how they
stayed up; now I was actually inside one, preparing to be
launched into the skies.

All I knew about Bill was that he was a senior executive in one of the big tobacco companies, but I had no idea if that meant he was rich or not by American standards. The world he was showing me seemed rich, but I had no idea how much things like airline tickets cost, no way of comparing it to anything I was used to. I just followed him around, like a wide-eyed child, doing what he told me, soaking up each new experience as it came, trying to make sense of it all.

As the plane took off I looked down on the city that had seemed so frightening and confusing when I first arrived in its streets. From the sky it looked like a toy town, completely unthreatening and manageable. It was as if I'd grown and the city had shrunk beneath me, and then it was gone and we were above the clouds in a world of our own, cocooned from reality, being waited on hand and foot. During the journey we must have moved through time zones, but I had no idea. It was all like a dream anyway and time was irrelevant. I'd entered a different world, never mind a different time zone.

All through the trip Bill was assuring me there was nothing to worry about, that I would be okay because he would look after me and make sure I was safe and comfortable. He was so kind and considerate. I just wished I fancied him, even a little bit. Imagine how it would have been to be on such an adventure with Jun and Dailyn.

'I've got a few girls living in the house,' he said, 'so you'll have company when I'm working.'

I wondered what he meant by 'a few girls'. Was it going to be the same as the first night I met him? Was I going to have to watch him having sex with other people? I was a little worried, but not really frightened because he was always so kind and respectful towards me. It wasn't till we got to the house that I discovered the 'girls' were servants in the house. He also had three or four boys working in his stables, looking after his horses. All the staff were American. Everything was so big, with so much space. In the kitchen giant fridges and freezers were packed with food and there were always rooms I could go to where I could be alone, watching television or just staring at the views.

Bill, it turned out, was a lot richer than I'd imagined. His house was a ranch on the outskirts of the city, and he introduced me to the staff as his friend. They all seemed to like him as an employer and they all went out of their way to be kind to me, realising I was a long way from home. They called me 'Ma'am' and did things like bringing me breakfast in bed, making it seem as if they actually wanted to spoil me rather than that they were doing as they were told. Having spent my life serving others I didn't feel comfortable being on the receiving end of it. There was no way I could ever have told anyone what to do and during the days, when Bill was out working, I would go around with the servants asking what I could do to help.

At the end of the week there was no talk of me going home, nor at the end of two weeks. The days were so pleasant they kept drifting by and before long I'd been in the house for five or six months. I tried to learn to ride, but I fell off and didn't have the nerve to get back on. It was such a long way to fall. We went into Manhattan quite a bit and he would buy me whatever I wanted. Mostly I just wanted to go on walks and stare up at the buildings. Every corner we turned presented me with a new view that took my breath away. He paid for me to have driving lessons, which I enjoyed, although I didn't go out on my own much, even once I'd managed to get a licence. There was nowhere I wanted to go. I was quite happy being around the house with the staff.

I shared a bedroom with Bill, so I guess the servants all assumed we were lovers, even though we weren't. He asked me a couple of times if we could make love, but I didn't want to, which must have been hard for him but he never complained. He had a lift from the kitchen to his bedroom so sometimes he would order food, just like in a hotel, and it would appear in the room as if by magic.

Whenever I talked to the servants about going back to the Philippines they'd all try to talk me into staying, telling me I made Bill happy by being there.

'I love you,' he told me on several occasions and I know he wanted me to tell him I felt the same, but I couldn't.

'I'd like you to stay here and marry me,' he announced one day.

He was such a nice a man and such a good friend, but I couldn't pretend I loved him when I didn't. Sometimes I wished I could be like some of the girls I'd met in Manila, who would have been able to pretend to love him in order to get what they wanted, but I could never have done that.

He kept taking me shopping and buying me jewellery or anything I wanted, but I felt less and less comfortable. All he wanted to do was please me.

'I'm sorry,' I said to him one day. 'I can't bear seeing you trying to please me like this. You're so nice and I don't want you to think I'm taking advantage of you. It's just not me.'

'Why?' he asked. 'What have I done wrong?'

'Nothing. You're the most wonderful man. You're the man of my dreams the way you treat me. But I don't have the right feelings for you. I wish I did.'

'I'll do anything for you,' he pleaded. 'Whatever happens I'll wait for you.'

'No,' I said. 'I just want a simple life.'

'Do you want to go back to your family? We can fly there every week if you want.'

'No,' I said, 'I'm sorry. I must go home to Manila now.'

I could see his heart was broken and he would cry whenever we talked about it. I wished I could do something for him.

'You'll find someone else,' I said, 'someone who can love you back.'

'No,' he shook his head, 'I'll never marry now. I thought I'd found the right person. There won't be anyone else. Anytime you want to come and visit you'll always be welcome. If you find someone to love and you start a family, bring them to visit me, please. Promise me you will?'

'Okay,' I said. 'I promise.'

Bill flew back to the Philippines with me and my family never even knew I'd been out of the country. I'd sent them money and phoned them a few times over the months, once I'd worked out the time differences, but they'd never asked me where I was calling from. Maybe Dad didn't want to think about it.

When we arrived in Manila we went to a hotel for one last night together. Bill must have been terribly unhappy, knowing the end was so close, and I felt desperately sad for him. But I was excited at the same time at the thought of seeing my family and friends. He had an appointment to go to the next day, so while he was out I went home to Beth. She didn't ask where I'd been, she'd just assumed I'd been with a customer. In the Philippines people are used to family members disappearing off on contracts at a moment's notice and returning a few months later, their pockets bulging with money. I'd let her know I was safe and that was enough for her. She didn't want to know the details.

There would be times when I would regret the decision to leave New York, when I would think it might be better to be with someone who loves you than to hope to find someone who you can love. But at that stage I wasn't ready to give up the search for true love, not yet. I wanted to find someone who would make me feel the way Jun had made me feel when I first met him. I didn't want to settle for someone who would just be a good friend to me.

CHAPTER NINE

Meeting Paul

Paul Donald saw me first when I was dancing at Jools. I was 19 years old by then and quite confident on stage. He asked the Mama San to invite me to his table. The first thing I noticed about him as I went over was that he was wearing jogging shorts, trainers and a t-shirt, which was unusual in a smart club. Most of the customers made a bit of an effort to dress up for their tropical evenings out. He was about 40 years old, fair skinned, slim and six foot three inches tall which meant he towered over me when he stood up. He had the sweetest, friendliest face I'd ever seen and I felt instantly comfortable in his company. I said yes when he asked if I would like to come out with him. When we got to his hotel room he was really charming, asking me all sorts of questions about my life and showing a genuine interest in my answers.

He told me he was divorced and worked as an electrical engineer for Shell in Brunei, which was another place I'd heard of but couldn't have placed on a map. As the hours passed he behaved like a perfect gentleman and in the end it was me who asked first whether he wanted to have sex, feeling an unusually strong attraction to him.

'Not really,' he said, 'It's just nice to have someone to talk to.'

'I have a condom in my bag if you need it,' I added, wondering if that was the reason he was hesitating.

He laughed at my eagerness, making me blush, but he didn't take me up on the offer, being happy just to kiss and cuddle. I was quite disappointed, but at the same time impressed by his politeness. I stayed in the room for the night and the next morning he told me he had to go out to meet some friends.

'Will you wait here for me to come back?' he asked.

'Okay,' I agreed, feeling a strong urge to see him again. I didn't imagine that staying in a luxury hotel room all day would be a hardship either.

But time hangs heavily in hotel rooms when you have nothing to do, however luxurious they are. None of the television channels really interested me and there was a limit to how long I could entertain myself in the bath. Used to always being busy, I looked around for something to do and noticed a pile of Paul's dirty clothes in the corner of the wardrobe. I decided to do his laundry and went out to a nearby shop to buy some soap. At the same time I bought some doughnuts and cakes for him when he came home, in case he hadn't had a chance to eat and was hungry.

Once I was back in the room I hand washed all his shirts and underclothes, hanging them out to dry in front of the electric fan in the room. It already felt like I'd known Paul for a long time, as if we were already a couple in some way.

All the chores done, I went back to waiting, staring out of the window or at the images that floated meaninglessly across the television screen. Outside it grew dark and the lights began to flicker on in the surrounding buildings. It was time for me to be getting back to work at the club and I had no idea when Paul would return; maybe he would be gone several days or more, I had no way of knowing. I left a note, telling him I wasn't able to wait any longer, and on the way out I asked the security guard to inform Mr Donald I was sorry to have missed him.

Paul must have arrived back at the hotel a few minutes after I'd left, and on finding me gone he took a taxi straight to the club to look for me.

'I want that girl back,' he told the Mama San as soon as he'd confirmed I was there.

I was talking to another customer at the time, a man who was already asking me to go out. The Mama San whispered in my ear that Paul was back and wanted to talk to me. I finished my drink and asked the other customer to excuse me for a moment. Before I'd even reached his table, Paul had paid the bar fine and was ready to leave.

'Go and get changed,' he told me. 'We're going out.'

I tried not to show quite how pleased I was to see him.

We went back to the hotel for a meal and he told me how worried he'd been that he might have lost me.

'No,' I said, 'you haven't lost me. I waited as long as I could.'

'I know, I'm sorry. The friend I went to meet was actually my pen pal. It was the first time I'd met her, even though we've been writing letters for a long time. I'd been planning to ask her if she would like to come back to Brunei with me.'

He pulled out a picture of a girl and showed it to me.

'What did she say?' I asked.

'She said she didn't have any feelings for me,' he admitted. 'All she wanted was for me to take her and her whole family shopping. I thought they would never finish. I missed you so much, I was thinking about you all day.'

As we continued to talk he told me he was due to go back to his job in Brunei the next day.

'I can't take you with me this time,' he said, 'but if you're a good girl I'll come back for you and take you next time.'

'Are you serious?' After the trip to New York I was eager for another new experience, especially if it was with this man who I fancied so much.

'Of course,' he assured me and I felt it was possible he might be sincere. I was so comfortable with him; it was as if we'd known each other in the past and had just been reunited. He was the perfect gentleman and made me feel special all the time. Whatever was happening in my heart wasn't the same overwhelming passion I'd felt when I first saw Jun, but there was something there that made me feel good in his company and I hoped it would grow. At the same time I wasn't completely sure if he was serious, knowing he'd spent the day with this pen pal. It seemed a funny thing for a man of his age to be doing, but then I was discovering new things about life every day, so maybe this was just one more of those things.

That night we made love for the first time and it was the best thing that had happened to me since I'd been parted from Jun. The following day I went with him to the airport to see him off. As I waved him goodbye I found I was unable to stop the tears from coming to my eyes. Something deep inside me had responded to Paul. I hardly dared to call it love, for fear I would end up as badly hurt as before.

I didn't allow myself to rely on his promise to come back. I was sure he meant it at the time, but once he'd been back in Brunei for a while I thought it was likely the memory of me would grow dimmer and he would meet other girls. I hoped with all my heart I would see him again, but I couldn't risk relying on it. I went back to work at the club, trying to put Paul out of my mind.

A few days later I received a letter from Brunci. Inside it was some money and a photograph of Paul looking very sexy on his motorbike. In the accompanying letter he told me how he was falling for me and how he would like to take me to this place and that place. I had to read his words several times before I could fully believe them. I wanted to write back to him but my English was still bad, so I asked my brother-in-law to help me find the right words.

When another letter arrived a couple of days later I thought it would be from Paul again, but to my amazement I discovered, on tearing it open, that it was from Jun. All the memories came flooding back as I read his words. He too had enclosed a picture of himself on a motorbike. It was as if the fates were deliberately playing with my emotions, trying to mix me up and confuse me about what I wanted and what I could have. In his letter Jun asked me to go back to him so that we could try to start again. It was the letter I'd been praying to receive for three or more years and now it had arrived it felt as if it was too late. I still loved Jun, but I'd finally stopped thinking about him all the time.

On my last trip home to visit my family I'd spotted Jun from a distance, and even a glimpse had set my pulse racing. I asked my cousin to go and talk to him on my behalf, not wanting to frighten him by going too close myself.

'Ask if I can visit him and Dailyn,' I instructed.

Jun sent back the message that I shouldn't bother to try to see them any more. His words had broken my heart all over again. I didn't want to dig up all that pain again, just when my heart was starting to heal.

It seemed possible I'd found a way to be happy again without him, then his letter arrived out of the blue, saying he'd changed his mind and wanted me back. I cried to think I finally had a chance to get Dailyn back, but it was going to be at too great a cost to my own soul. It was with a mixture of terrible sadness and some satisfaction that I replied to his letter in the same tone he had once written to me, telling him that he must forget about me, that it was all over. It was agony for me to write the words but I also wanted him to feel exactly as I had when I'd read and heard his words of rejection. I'd loved him so much and I don't know if I would have had the strength to write that letter if I hadn't known I had Paul to turn to and that I had a chance of happiness with him. If Jun's letter had come a few weeks earlier I might have reacted very differently and we might all have been spared the terrible chain of events that was to come. But who ever knows what the gods hold in store for us?

Over the next two weeks Paul wrote to me three more times, his letters bubbling with enthusiasm for things we could do together in the future and I grew more and more confident I'd made the right decision. He sent me enough money so that I never needed to go out with any more customers, keeping myself just for him. By the time he came back to Manila a few months later he'd arranged a visitor's visa for me to travel to Brunei and I knew for sure he was serious.

I had no idea what to expect as I got off the plane in Brunei, a tiny kingdom in Northern Borneo. Just 800 miles from Manila, Brunei is still ruled by a Sultan, one of the richest men in the world. When we left the airport my first impression was of green, stretching away in all directions, as we drove past miles of well-watered grass along the smooth new roads leading towards Paul's house. Compared to the haphazard chaos and shabbiness of Manila everything was so clean and new looking, as if the whole country had been buffed up and manicured with oil money.

Beneath the glossy surface, however, life in Brunei was not that different from the Philippines, partly because there were so many Filipinas living there, working as everything from maids to lawyers as well as married to Bruneians. Paul lived in the capital city, Bandar Seri Begawan. On my first day he took me to his office at Shell and introduced me to his colleagues. As I shook them all by the hand I felt proud that he was so happy to show me off. None of them knew that he'd picked me out in a bar in Manila; they all assumed we'd met in Brunei and we said nothing to correct them.

Because so many people come and go in Brunei on short-term contracts, people are very welcoming and friendly to newcomers. It wasn't long before neighbours started introducing themselves. There were always lots of parties and social gatherings where everyone talked and I found I had a wide circle of friends within just a few weeks of arriving. Some of them, I realised, were superficial, but one or two of them grew to be close within a surprisingly short time and I was able to spend as much time with them as I wanted. I thought I could be very happy in such a place, living with such a good man.

Paul's house was massive, and just as immaculate as everything else in Brunei – not a thing out of place, everything new and clean and orderly, as if it had just been unwrapped. He had a maid to keep everything polished and it all felt so perfect to me compared to life in the Philippines. I loved the sense of calm and order and comfort. I wondered if I'd reached the place that was my destiny. I felt so comfortable and happy. It wasn't quite the same explosion of love that I'd felt when I first met Jun, but it was still a wonderful feeling. In a way it was nicer because I could relax and breathe easily. Being completely infatuated can be frightening and exhausting. I wondered if it was just that I'd finally grown up and this was what grown-up love was meant to be like; not passionate and overwhelming, but pleasant and safe and comforting. I did love Paul, but somehow I couldn't quite bring myself to say it to him, even when he said it to me. Love can be the hardest word to say.

Paul had achieved exactly the sort of life he wanted and perhaps I should have questioned whether there would be space in it for another person. He was very well paid, sometimes earning as much as £13,000 a month, and all his material needs were taken care of. The house was lovely, he had a BMW, which I soon learned to drive, as well as the motorbike, and he had plenty of friends. I felt as if I had crossed over into the world that I had first encountered in the hotel rooms of the men I met at Jools.

I was now able to find the money my family needed to finish their stone house. For so long I had dreamed of being able to do such a thing, and finally it had become a reality.

It was a single-storey house in Panlayaan, set in a hill-side jungle clearing and surrounded by a seven-foot wall. Determined to make it as solid as possible, we built it on a three-foot-thick reinforced concrete float and the roof and walls were interconnected steel reinforced slabs. Wrought iron framework was fitted to all windows for security and to prevent flying debris from smashing the windows during storms.

The outside walls were painted white while inside we painted everything bright, cheerful colours. At the front of the house we built a marble-tiled veranda with white balustrades, so that the family could sit on bamboo chairs on fine evenings and watch the world go by. The main bedroom, with its marble-tiled floor and two bay win-dows was big enough to sleep up to nine people, while the second bedroom at the rear of the house was for Mama and Papa to have for themselves. There was also a bathroom and a living room, which was the biggest room in the house, divided from the clean kitchen by a screen made from wood from Papa's land. I was so pleased they were finally secure. I was even able to buy my mother household goods to make her life easier.

Initially the only thing that made me uneasy about life with Paul was finding a lot of women's clothes hanging in one of his wardrobes. They were all small enough to fit me, so there was no chance they belonged to him! When I asked him about them he dismissed my fears, telling me they belonged to a girl he'd once known. He was so open and unconcerned about me finding them that I decided not to pursue the subject any further. I could hardly hope to move into the life of a middle-aged man and not expect to find there had been a few other women in his past. In fact it would have been a bit suspicious if there hadn't been any.

It was so easy to live with Paul that on the surface I was contented nearly all the time, so contented in fact that I sometimes became bored with the lack of drama in my life. Because the maid was there to do the housework and because I didn't have to earn a living, I had all day long to please myself; shopping, cooking if I didn't feel like eating out, or going out to other people's houses, socialising and making new friends. The trouble with having so much spare time, however, was that it gave me space to think about Dailyn and how much I missed her. The sadness was always there, beneath the surface, waiting to rise up.

To begin with I only had a two-week visa and had to travel back to the Philippines every fortnight to renew it. Each time I was there I would spend a few days with Mum, which was the most time we'd spent together since I was ill. She was so happy to think I'd found a man who would look after me well and take me away from the bar life in Manila.

On one of my visits home I went to show my face to my aunt in Sorsogon. I wanted her to see just how far her little servant girl had gone since I worked for her. I wore all the jewellery I owned, sprayed myself liberally with an expensive smelling perfume and put on my best clothes. I looked brilliant, even if I say so myself. She seemed surprised to find me on the doorstep, too surprised to even find an excuse to turn me away.

'So!' Auntie said, once we were sitting in her house, drinking tea. 'I hear you've built a stone house in Panlayaan?'

'Yes,' I said, unable to stop myself from beaming proudly.

We chatted on for a little longer as she pretended to be interested in the health and welfare of my family, and I in hers. Then she changed the subject.

'Do you think, Gina, you could lend me some five six?'

She meant that if I lent her some money, she was willing to pay back 600 peso for every 500 she borrowed. I'd
been waiting for this moment for years. I had not forgotten the way she'd treated me when I worked for her and
her family.

'Do you remember,' I said, as if reminiscing pleasant-
ly, 'when I was a child, how I said to you once, "one day
maybe I will be able to help you, Auntie"?'

'I'm not sure I remember that,' she replied, looking a
little flustered, unsure what might be coming next.

'You said, "What could you ever do for me Gina? You
dream too much, now get on with your work." And now
you are asking for my help.'

I let my words sink in for a moment or two. I knew I
was gloating, but I didn't care. I'd imagined a million
times how it would feel to one day speak back to her.

'I'm afraid, Auntie,' I said eventually, 'that although I
would love to help, I only have enough for my family.'

She accepted the news with a curt nod. I guess it was
all just 'business' to her, nothing personal. My rejection of
her request certainly didn't seem to have any effect on
the rest of her family. Once they knew I had money all
her daughters started being nice to me, asking for perfume and presents.

'I treat people,' I told them, 'how they treat me.'

I always took presents back with me and some of Dad's
relatives seemed to be envious of my good fortune and
eager to undermine it. One of my uncle's wives spread

rumours behind my back that I was only in Manila and that I was making it up about travelling abroad. I didn't bother to argue. What did it matter what they thought? One day a friend asked if I really had been abroad and if they could see my passport. I was happy to show them.

I felt sad that even though I was doing my best to help the family in every way I could, there were still people who wanted to complain and say I didn't do enough. I thought perhaps they were just jealous, so I didn't blame them, but it took away some of the pleasure of my new good fortune. If I took back 50 bars of chocolate there were always 51 people who thought they should have some. Every branch of the family had so many children and cousins it was hard to please all of them all the time.

The women in my family all work very hard from the day they're able to help around the house as children. They never have days off or weekends away. If my clothes and shoes became worn I could now go to the shops and replace them. When my sisters' clothes and shoes became worn they had to walk around barefoot and in rags, preferring to spend what little money they had on their children. Whenever I went home I treated all of my sisters and tried to make them feel special, knowing what it felt like to have nothing.

My mother's younger sister was married to my father's younger brother. All my life the two sisters did nothing but fight. They used to live just one step from our house and if we cooked something nice for the family, with none to spare, my aunt would refuse to speak to any of us the next day. If we gave her some of our food, however, she was charming. She was always telling Mum she was greedy, only thinking about her own children. In the beginning I used to bring this aunt back presents on every visit and Mum told me off, saying that they didn't deserve them after the way they had treated us down the years.

'Look up there, Mama,' I said, pointing to the skies. 'He never sleeps. He's watching us, everyone.'

She smiled and hugged me, because she recognised her own words, the ones she used to use when I asked her why she put up with the way the rest of the family treated her.

On another return visit to the Philippines, Paul's mother, Jane, and his younger brother, David, came out from England to meet us for a Christmas holiday. She and I got on well and his brother was very sweet. I found myself calling Jane 'Mum' almost from the moment we met. Even though she was nearly 70 she was really lively and bubbly and wanted to go out on the town in the evenings. On New Year's Eve we took her and David to Jools to show her where Paul and I had met. She loved it, dancing with all the girls. Everyone laughed at the sight of an old lady enjoying herself in such a place. All the girls I had worked with were there and greeted me like a long-lost sister. It felt strange, being there as a customer.

'It's nice here, Gina,' Jane shouted over the music.

The girls were crowding round Paul and we tried to fix David up with one of them, a girl called Rona. They exchanged addresses and everything and a few weeks after getting back to England David received a letter from her saying she wanted to keep in touch. He didn't respond. I don't think he was that bothered with girls, being quite happy living on his own.

Their mum was having such a good time at the club she ended up falling over on the stairs, but didn't do herself any damage.

Eventually I managed to get my passport stamped with a permanent visa for Brunei and I didn't have to go back to the Philippines so often, I could just send the family money and gifts instead.

When Paul asked me to marry him, about a year after I first came to Brunei, I barely hesitated before I said yes. I would never have married someone if I didn't love them and I was confident of my feelings for him, even if I couldn't put them into words. When I accepted his proposal he was so happy he bought me a holiday home on a beach in a Philippine resort. I was shocked by such a generous gift.

'You don't have to do that,' I protested.

'I want to show you how much I love you,' he insisted.

'You don't have to buy me anything to show me that.'

But he wouldn't take any argument and it felt good to know he loved me so much. Despite my nagging sadness over missing Dailyn, I felt a contentment I hadn't experienced since I was a tiny child, when I didn't understand where problems came from. Because I'd been able to give my family enough money to build their stone house and meet all their needs I had no worries about them either. It was a good time.

Paul had always said he didn't think he wanted to be a father and I could see that having children would disrupt the organised, peaceful life he had constructed for himself as a bachelor. As it was, he could do exactly what he pleased and there was no one messing up his beautiful house while he was out at work. But when I told him that taking the pill was making me sick and giving me skin complaints, he didn't hesitate to suggest I should come off it. I was pretty sure I wouldn't be able to conceive again after everything my body had gone through during my illness after the birth of Dailyn.

Paul seemed very relaxed about the whole thing, even when I had to tell him I'd fallen pregnant. I was scared what his reaction would be, but once I realised he wasn't going to make a fuss I was overjoyed. At last I was going to have another chance at being a mother, and I could feel confident I was bringing my baby into a safe, secure life, with plenty of money for all the necessities. It was a wonderful feeling, although it did also remind me even more of how much I missed Dailyn. I would imagine how great it would be to have her with me as I produced her new baby brother or sister, and it made me feel sad for everything both she and I were missing.

There were also moments when I worried I might become as ill after the birth of the new baby as I'd been after having Dailyn. I couldn't bear the thought of losing my mind again and then returning to sanity to find that Paul and the baby had been taken from me, just as Jun and Dailyn had been.

Shortly before the day of our wedding I answered the phone in the house and a girl's voice asked for Paul.

'He's not here,' I said in my national language. I could tell from her accent she was from the Philippines. 'But you can contact him at his office. Who's speaking?'

'Who's this?' she asked, suspiciously.

'I'm the helper,' I lied. 'Who am I speaking to?'

'It's nothing to do with you.'

'Okay,' I said, as sweetly as I could manage. 'I'll give you Paul's number.'

She then blurted out that she was calling because she was not well and needed some money. When Paul got home from work I asked if this woman had managed to get hold of him.

'Yeah,' he said, casually. 'She was asking about you. I think she was a bit jealous.'

I didn't like the idea that he was in touch with a woman from his past, but I did like the idea that he was a kind man and would help an old friend if she needed it.

So I said nothing. A few days later she rang again, knowing now that I was Paul's new girlfriend, and became quite nasty. We then received a letter from the Philippines. It was from the same woman and she had inserted a photograph of herself. She was asking for money again.

'What do you think I should do?' Paul asked, as if this was a problem we could solve together.

'I can't help you,' I said. 'You knew her before I came into your life, so you must decide.'

'I don't think I'll bother,' he said and inside I gave a sigh of relief. I wrote back to her, enclosing the photograph and saying I was sorry but that we wouldn't be able to help. I also told her we were going to be getting married, to make sure there wouldn't be any more misunderstandings.

We had to annul my marriage to Jun, which wasn't hard as I'd been below the legal age when the wedding took place, and I was two or three months pregnant by the time Paul and I got married in a registry office, with a party for about a hundred friends afterwards. It was a nice day and I wore a knee-length cream dress with sequins round the front. I enjoyed myself but I wished my family could have been there, as they had been for my first wedding. I had invited them, but my parents didn't like the idea of travelling abroad and the cost of bringing over all the other relatives was too great. Paul's family wasn't able to come over from England either, so the day was more like a normal Brunei party than a family celebration.

Paul's contract with Shell had finished just before I became Mrs Donald, which meant he had to find another house and another job, but it didn't seem to worry him. Most of the expatriates working in Brunei were on short contracts and constantly moving around, living a bit like affluent gypsies. It didn't dent our happiness one bit as we looked forward to the next big event, the birth of our baby.

CHAPTER TEN

Baby Troubles

As he expected, it didn't take long for Paul to find another electrical engineering job and another house very similar to the first one. I guess he must have been good at whatever it was he did. Experts like him seemed to be in great demand in Brunei, able to walk from one contract to another without any trouble. After a few anxious weeks for me, our lifestyle was back to where it had been, which meant very comfortable indeed.

When I was five months pregnant we decided to travel to Liverpool in England to visit Jane and the rest of Paul's family. I was looking forward to seeing them again and visiting England, my husband's country. We stayed with Jane in the family home, which was very pleasant. I think Paul's father had been an attorney and Jane had been a nurse, so there had never been any shortage of money in Paul's childhood. Paul and I came from two such different backgrounds, but we lived together in a sort of no-man's land in Brunei, where so many people were severed from their roots, both of us foreigners. In England, however, I was most definitely the odd one out.

Although my English was getting much better, I still had difficulty with some of the slang words people used, and I didn't take to the weather. It was wintertime and I'd never been cold before. I also missed the food I was used to. None of this, however, could dent my happiness at being the wife of a nice man and an expectant mother, living as part of a loving family.

Inevitably there were some gaps between our cultures, which led to misunderstandings.

'Are you all right, pet?' Jane asked me one morning and I didn't understand why she would be calling me an animal.

'What have I done to upset Mum?' I asked Paul later, having been brooding on the insult for some hours.

'Why do you think you've upset her?' he asked, obviously surprised since he thought we were getting on so well.

'She called me "pet" this morning.'

'No,' he laughed, 'it means she likes you, don't worry.'

Although I was thrilled to be pregnant I was also worried. I was getting the same stomach pains I'd experienced with Dailyn, and both Paul and I were nervous about things going wrong in my head and body like they had the last time. I didn't want to end up back in the hands of witch doctors and faith healers and thought it would be better to have my baby in England if possible. Paul agreed.

Michael eventually arrived at the end of March 1995, just as spring was starting to break through. I was 22 years old. He was ten days late, but well worth the wait. He was a beautiful child and immediately became the love of my life. I could hardly believe I had a healthy baby and still felt well enough to look after him. No one was going to be able to take this one away from me. It was like a dream come true. I was so relieved not to be feeling ill again.

'I'm so pleased Paul has found you,' Jane told me one day. 'This is the happiest I have ever seen him. You will look after him for me, won't you?'

'Yes,' I said, 'I definitely will look after him. We love each other, that's all that matters.'

'That's all I want to hear.'

Once Michael was three weeks old we flew back to the Philippines to introduce him to my mum. We then spent a few weeks in Singapore for Paul's work, before going back home to Brunei. Apart from some headaches that I didn't seem to be able to shake off, my life couldn't have been any better. Having Paul and Michael to look after made me completely happy. We travelled a lot together and I even took them both to meet Bill in New York, as I'd promised him I would. Bill was just as sweet as I remembered and seemed genuinely pleased I'd kept my promise to bring my family to stay with him.

Paul changed jobs again soon after Michael's birth and we moved to yet another house in the city, this time a massive one with five bedrooms and five bathrooms.

We had another helper in the house so I still had to do hardly any housework and I wanted to do more than just sit around all day. I had been on a fashion course, which I enjoyed, but I needed to be doing more. I asked Paul if he would mind if I worked. There were still a lot of things I wanted to do for my family and I didn't like having to ask him for all the money. He thought it was a good idea and helped me get a job as a waitress at one of the big hotels which was owned by someone connected to the royal family. It was nice to be busy again and to be earning my own money. On the days I was working, Paul would sometimes take Michael with him. Sometimes the two of them would come into the hotel to visit me between shifts.

Our helper would also look after Michael if both of us were working at the same time. She and I got on well, although she never wanted anyone else to know that I was her boss. For some reason, many Filipinos don't mind working for foreigners but they think there's something shameful about working for other Filipinos. If we were out with Michael in a pushchair and she saw any of her friends she would quickly pass the pushchair to me. She used to call Paul 'Sir' and me 'Gina'.

Mostly I didn't mind, though, because she was a good friend to me and I never felt comfortable giving her instructions anyway. But sometimes it was hard because I needed something specific done and she wouldn't accept being told what to do by me. Paul kept telling me I was the boss and I had to tell her what to do. He couldn't understand why it made me feel so bad. If I really wanted her to do something I would get him to ask her for me.

One day I took Michael swimming all day. When we got back I asked her if she could cook something for Paul, while I made a meal for us.

'I've been very tired all day,' she protested, 'and now you're asking me to cook?'

With that she stormed off to her room, slammed the door and locked it. When Paul came home I explained what had happened. He knocked on her door, asking her to open it. She refused and we could hear her crying on the inside. To my surprise Paul kicked the door open. It was the first time I'd seen him lose his temper and I was shocked. He'd always been so gentle and polite, but now I could see there was a limit to his patience and understanding. I hoped he would never become angry with me.

She didn't last much longer after that and the replacement we found didn't have the same hang-ups, becoming a true friend as well as a helper. Sometimes she and I would talk so much Paul would become irritated.

'Why do you spend so much time talking to a maid?' he would want to know.

'She's my friend,' I'd protest. 'I don't care if she's a maid or not.'

I'd been a servant myself for enough years to know that it doesn't make you a different species.

I was enjoying my job at the hotel, feeling busy and useful again, but the head of the catering division, who was a Canadian, made it obvious he fancied me. He began to make my life a bit uncomfortable, telling me he didn't want my family visiting me in the hotel because it made him jealous. There would also be times when he would send everyone else home and ask me to stay on for some reason, or he would make personal comments about how tiny my figure was, or he would save special bits of food for me and be offended if I didn't eat them and show sufficient gratitude. It made me feel very awkward, but I didn't want to give up the job. Not only did I like the work, the wages were allowing me to send more money to my family without bothering Paul all the time. I kept going without saying anything, hoping he would get the hint and give up.

When we heard that Jane had breast cancer, which had spread to her lungs, and was only likely to live for a few months, we wanted to return to England to be with her. Even though Michael was only about 18 months old, I hoped that perhaps this would leave him with some memory of his grandmother. I assured my boss I would come back to work when I returned to Brunei, but I didn't think I really wanted to.

When we reached England Jane was already in a hospice. She was so pleased to see us.

'It's so sad,' she said as she cuddled Michael. 'I finally have a grandchild and now I'm dying.'

I didn't know what to say, her words made me want to cry. They made me wonder how long it would be before I would be reunited with Dailyn.

Because of Paul's job we were only able to stay a few weeks, but we knew we would be coming back to England again soon because Jane was becoming very weak. It was an emotional parting, all three of us aware that it might be the last time we would meet.

When I returned to Brunei I didn't contact the hotel, not feeling like going back to work for the Canadian man and putting up with all the harassment again. A week or two later I received a call from someone more senior than him, asking why I hadn't come to work. I didn't want him to think badly of me, so I told him the truth. I later heard that the Canadian had been sacked, but I still didn't feel like going back. It was time to move on and think of something else to do. As he was growing older and more mobile, Michael was becoming more time-consuming and in need of a mother's attention.

An old friend of Paul's, a teacher called Brian, got in touch with him one day and they started talking about getting together a rock band. Paul was a good drummer but he hadn't had a group to play in very often while we were travelling and moving from one house to another. Having been around a great deal while Michael was a tiny baby, he now wanted a bit more freedom to get back to his old bachelor habits with Brian. In fact, he wanted to be out every evening, practising or playing his music. I didn't mind because I was happy for him to have a hobby and I was also happy to have time alone with Michael. I had plenty of friends of my own to visit or invite round if I got lonely, and I had my helper to talk to. I also invited my sister Sonia to stay for a while to give her a taste of a different lifestyle from the one she was used to in the Philippines.

Although he had enjoyed having a new baby, as Michael got bigger and more inquisitive Paul's patience seemed to wear thin very easily. Maybe he had been a bachelor too long and was too set in his ways to be able to adapt to the changes that a child inevitably brings to a home and its routines. A healthy toddler makes a lot of noise and can't just be quietened down with a bottle or a sleep. Michael was very active and always sticking his fingers into things around the house, like hi-fis and electronic equipment. I had to keep my eye on him the whole time, and even then there were times when my attention would be distracted and he would be into something else by the time I looked back. Paul's temper was becoming shorter and shorter every day and he started to smack Michael much too hard whenever he displeased him, leaving ugly red marks. There is no way you can hide a toddler from his father when they're both in the same house, and I lived in growing fear of Paul's explosions, relieved whenever he went out with his friends.

Yet somehow Paul would always make it seem that whatever he had done was justified, after the event. He was very good at making me think it was my fault. If he had obviously gone too far he would apologise and would promise it would never happen again. Most of the time our lives together were happy and I couldn't bring myself to break up Michael's family as long as I thought there was a chance things would get better.

When I look back I can see clearly that I should have immediately taken Michael home to the Philippines and refused to return, but things seemed different. Paul was usually so charming and whenever it happened I thought this would be the last time anything bad would happen. Breaking up a family when you have a child is such a big step to take; I just couldn't bring myself to do it, especially when I already had one broken marriage and one lost child. I thought I was strong enough to stand up for myself and protect Michael. I thought things would get better once Michael was older and easier to control. I made a hundred excuses to myself why we were better off with Paul than without him.

When the explosions did happen I found I couldn't stand by and watch my baby being smacked and so Paul and I began to argue fiercely. His temper would then transfer from Michael to me. Our fights often ended in him slapping me or pulling me around the room by my hair in his efforts to shut me up. I'd never seen this side of his character when it was just the two of us, when he had nothing to interfere with his organised, comfortable life. One night he became so exasperated he picked me up and threw me across the room onto the bed with such force that it snapped beneath me. The next day the helper, whose room was directly below ours, asked what the loud noise in the night had been.

'Oh,' I said vaguely, 'I just fell over the bed.'

I never wanted to tell anyone, not even her, what was happening, because I didn't want them to think badly of Paul. He was my husband and the father of my child, I wanted them to go on believing he was this nice guy they all met at parties or at work. To admit I was in an abusive marriage would have been like admitting to fail-ure. I was determined to deal with it on my own.

At the time I had just become pregnant again, because Paul had said he thought Michael should have a little brother or sister, and the next day, to my horror, I found I was bleeding. I called Paul at work to tell him. He took me to the hospital to see Dr Reynolds who was a good friend of his, as well as being our family doc-tor.

'I'm sorry,' Dr Reynolds said, after examining me. 'The baby has died.'

The next day they operated to remove the foetus and the doctor asked me what I thought might have caused the problem.

'I don't know,' I lied, avoiding his eyes. 'Maybe I'm just overtired.'

Something in his manner told me he wasn't convinced by my answer, but he decided not to probe any further and I still didn't feel I should be disloyal to my husband, particularly as Dr Reynolds was his friend.

Paul didn't seem to like coming home any more, preferring to stay out with his friends until long after I had gone to bed. I didn't mind how much time he spent out, as long as he didn't hit Michael or me and shout at us when he came back. He thought I was being overprotective and that Michael needed to be taught right from wrong, but I didn't think there was ever a reason to hit a small child. Michael wasn't particularly naughty or difficult, just inquisitive and full of energy.

It seemed that Paul was looking for reasons to argue. He'd always been fussy about his food, so usually I would cook something especially for him because the helper didn't know quite how he liked everything. But he kept complaining. Whenever I'd made a meal he would say he wasn't hungry because he'd already eaten, or had already arranged to go out. Nothing I did would please him. We seemed to be wasting so much food all the time I stopped bothering to prepare meals for him, but that made him even madder.

Soon he was staying out till two or three every morning, but I didn't question him about where he'd been. Despite his ill-tempered behaviour at home I still trusted him. I felt he was mature enough not to need to be playing around with other women. I convinced myself that he'd got all that sort of thing out of his system as a young man, which was why he had decided to marry me and settle down with a family. Some nights, when he did eventually come in, he would fall asleep on the sofa and by the time I woke up I would find him already dressed for work and eating his breakfast in the kitchen. If I asked him why he hadn't come to bed he'd say it was because he didn't want to disturb me, and would then leave the house as quickly as possible before I could ask any more questions.

When I'd met him he'd had no interest in clothes, something I realised the first night I saw him in shorts, t-shirt and trainers. But his scruffy appearance made him look older than he actually was, so I took care of buying his clothes and laying them out for him, making sure he was always well turned out before he left the house. I'd had a lot of training in laundry work over the years and he looked at least ten years younger by the time I'd finished with him.

But now I noticed he'd become more concerned about such things himself, as if his appearance had suddenly become important.

'Do I look okay?' he'd ask, fussing around in front of the mirror before going out.

We were talking less and less and to make up for the silence between us I started entertaining more. I'd become friendly with the people working in the local department store and spent a lot of time socialising in their staff house. Every week I would throw a party to distract myself from the feeling that something was going wrong between us, and to hide from my sadness. If anyone else wanted a party and didn't have a venue for it I would volunteer our house: anything to keep myself busy and to fill my life with people. When it was Michael's birthday I invited around a hundred people to the house, most of them adults, to celebrate with us. There was a disco, a buffet and everything.

Michael was very popular with everyone because he was so cute, with long curly hair and big almond-shaped eyes. There was always a lot of drinking and smoking going on amongst my social group and I got swept along with all the bad habits of the expatriate lifestyle. Almost every night I would drink until I was unconscious. It helped me to keep up the pretence that there wasn't anything going wrong in my marriage.

Because Brunei is a Muslim state we weren't allowed to buy alcohol in the country, so we would go across the border into Malaysia and bring back the legal limit each time, stockpiling it in the house. So many people did it that there was always plenty of drink at every party.

Paul's friends were different to mine and didn't seem to like me much. I never got to know them that well but the ones I did speak to were usually engineers, technicians or teachers, people very like himself. Although they would say hello they would never really talk to me. It seemed as if they disapproved of me, but I couldn't work out what

I'd done to offend them. Maybe they thought I was trying to spoil his fun, being the nagging wife and mother.
I could never have told them the truth of what went on
between us because I don't think they would have
believed me, and I wouldn't have wanted them to think
badly of Paul.

When Jane died we went back to England for the
funeral. I was sad we hadn't been there for her at the end,
but Paul's new job had made it impossible. Jane had been
very kind to me, welcoming me into her family when she
could so easily have been judgemental, and I was sorry
Michael hadn't had a chance to get to know her better.
She must have been worried when she heard her son was
going to marry a bar girl from Manila, but she never for
a moment let me think she didn't love me like a daughter. I would always remember the night she came with us
to Jools and we were all so happy together.

I wanted to recapture that feeling, and put an end to
whatever it was that was coming between Paul and me,
growing bigger and uglier all the time. Anger was building up inside me at the way in which he seemed willing
to let things fall apart in our relationship without making
any effort, only ever wanting to spend time with his
friends.

One night, back in Brunei, when Paul came creeping
in at three o'clock in the morning after one of his nights
out, I plucked up my courage and cornered him in the
bathroom, asking him where he'd been.

'Oh, just around with friends,' he replied, vaguely, obviously not wanting to answer any questions.

'Why do you always have to stay out all the time?' I demanded.

My refusal to allow myself to be brushed aside seemed to infuriate him and his tone suddenly changed, becoming aggressive.

'At least I came home,' he snapped, as if he thought he was doing me a favour. 'If you're not happy with it then leave!'

'All right,' I said, calling his bluff, 'I'll go.'

'You're not taking Michael with you,' he warned.

'Of course I'm taking Michael with me!'

Not only was I not willing to be parted from my beloved son, there was no way I would be leaving him in the care of a father who smacked him whenever he was cross, and who was out all the time with God knew who. His temper erupted and he lashed out, grabbing my hair in his fist.

'You're not taking Michael,' he shouted, jerking my head about painfully. 'And if you ever try to take him you won't be going anywhere.'

Yanking myself free I ran out of the bathroom.

'You try taking him,' he shouted after me, 'and I'll be coming after you!'

The argument raged on around the house for a while and then subsided into a resentful silence between us. All the feelings I'd had of safety and security when I first married him had vanished; all the kindness and love he'd shown me at the beginning of our relationship had turned to anger and loathing.

'What's wrong with this stereo?' he asked me on one of his rare evenings in, as he tried to get the music to work.

'I don't know,' I said. 'Michael must have pressed one of the buttons.'

I regretted the words the moment they left my mouth.

'There are so many of you here,' he shouted. 'Why can't you control that child?'

Realising he was getting into one of his tempers I fell silent, hoping it would pass. He tried a few more times to make the stereo work, his fury building with each failed attempt, and then he exploded, grabbing the unsuspecting Michael and beating him all over his body. I snatched Michael from his grip, hugging his shaking body to me as he screamed and sobbed from a mixture of shock, pain and fear.

'Don't you dare hurt him like that!' I shouted.

'I can do what I like with my own son!' Paul roared back.

The next morning Michael was a mass of bruises and I knew we had to get away. As soon as Paul was out of the house I packed our things and we flew to the Philippines to be with my mother. I hadn't told my parents anything about the problems that had been growing between Paul and me because I didn't want them to have to worry about me again. I wanted to show them how I could manage my own life successfully, prove that I wasn't as lazy and useless as they had believed me to be. To have gone back and confessed my marriage was falling apart would have been an admission of defeat, especially when the first one had ended so disastrously, so I pretended this was just like any other visit.

While I was at home in the mountains I started to receive some anonymous letters, telling me what a terrible woman I was. I couldn't imagine who they were from. They'd been posted in the Philippines so I wondered if they were something to do with Jun's family. I had so many other things to think about I put them to the back of my mind, but it was unpleasant to think there was someone thinking these things about me.

Being there gave Michael a chance to get to know his grandparents and his cousins, and gave us both a break from Paul. I didn't give any thought to what we would do next, being too exhausted and confused to think about anything. After almost a month, Paul flew over and asked me to go back to him.

'We'll start again,' he promised. 'I'm sorry about the way I behaved. It won't happen again.'

I really wanted to repair the relationship and get back to how it had been when we first met and when we first had Michael, so I agreed. But once we were back in Brunei it was obvious nothing had changed; still he came home in the middle of the night and still we argued about everything. I was surprised by how quiet the helper was when I arrived back. She seemed not to want to look me in the eye or sit down and gossip in the kitchen as we had before I went away. I soon realised she must have been watching everything that was going on, trying to decide what was the right thing to do.

'Madam,' she said eventually, when we were alone one day, 'while you were away he had another girl here.'

I remembered a conversation Paul and I had had a while before, when he told me that his friend, Brian, was having an affair.

'Are you sure it's him,' I'd joked, 'and not you having this affair?'

He had laughed as if we both knew what a ridiculous suggestion that was. As I listened to her words now I realised I'd been a fool. It had been him all along. I was devastated.

All I wanted at first was for him to be honest with me, so that we could talk sensibly about what we were going to do. When I confronted him he denied it completely. He seemed so disappointed I would think such a thing of him that I actually ended up feeling guilty for being suspicious. But he still wasn't able to give a convincing explanation for the woman who had been at the house.

Although the atmosphere was still tense between us, we went to our holiday home for a break. One morning we visited an internet café because Paul wanted to send some emails. I could use a computer but I didn't know anything about the internet at the time, so I was watching over his shoulder as he typed in his password, 'Marietta'.

'Is that your password?' I asked, a terrible chill running through me and a knot forming in my stomach.

'You can use any name as long as it's eight letters,' he said, dismissively.

'So why didn't you use your own name or mine?'

'I never thought about it.'

'But why did you choose that name?'

'You can use anything that's memorable,' he repeated.

'So that woman's name is more memorable to you than ours?'

'Oh, just forget about it. It doesn't mean anything.'

'No.' I knew I would never be able to forget this. 'This is about the truth.'

'You're so paranoid.'

I left it at that stage, but it was still churning over and over in my head and I couldn't find any way to make it look better. I didn't bring the subject up again until we were back in Manila, waiting for our flight. We were in a hotel room and I started questioning him again. His temper exploded immediately and he punched me. I heard Michael screaming as I reeled back under the impact.

'If you can't take my word for it that there's nothing to worry about, then stay out of my life,' he shouted.

Cuddling Michael to me, I told him I was going to have to leave him because I couldn't stand it any more.

'Do what you like,' he said, 'as long as you leave Michael.'

'You know that isn't going to happen.'

I was so muddled I couldn't think what to do. I decided I would go back to Brunei to start with, to get my stuff together. The next day, in a taxi on the way to the airport, Michael started to cry. I guess he could pick up on the unhappy atmosphere between his parents, as children sometimes do, and Paul hit him on the legs to shut him up. Without thinking I hit him back and he punched me hard. I could see the taxi driver's shocked eyes watching us in the mirror. When we drew up at the airport Paul got out and stalked straight into the terminal without getting a trolley.

'Miss,' the driver whispered to me, 'if I was you I wouldn't go back with him, seeing the way he treats you both.'

The fact that he was kind enough to speak up, when he didn't have to say anything, made me cry. I thought about just driving away with him, but Paul had Michael's passport. I couldn't see that I had a choice at that stage. I had to organise things properly.

Back in Brunei his job ended again and we had to move out of the house, so I decided to stay with him until he was settled and hope things got better during that time. The only place we could find at short notice was the maid's quarters in a friend's house, not far from our old home. It wasn't much more than one room. My helper got pregnant and had to go back to the Philippines to give birth because she wasn't allowed to do it in Brunei. It was just as well, because there would have been nowhere for her to sleep in the flat.

It wasn't long before Paul got another job but it was an hour and a half's drive away from where we were living. All the uncertainty and stress added even more pressure to what was left of our relationship.

Alone in our cramped new home while Paul was at work, trying to make it comfortable, I pulled out an old toolbox of his as I needed some tools to repair the bed. When I opened it I found an envelope containing what felt like a ring. On the outside of the envelope were the words, 'I love you'. My heart was thumping and I was crying even before I opened it and what looked like a woman's engagement ring fell into my hand.

When I confronted him with it late that night he made up some excuse about a former girlfriend asking him to look after it for her, but it was obvious he was lying because initially he denied any knowledge of it at all. He tried to shrug the subject off in his usual style, but I couldn't stop myself from asking questions and gradually it came out that he'd met this woman since being married to me and had asked her to marry him.

'Just forget about the ring,' he said. 'It's all over. Give it to me and I'll throw it away.'

'Throwing it away won't allow me to forget about it,' I said. How would any woman be able to forget the fact that her husband has asked another woman to marry him?

I couldn't bear to be under the same roof as him for a moment longer so, even though it was the middle of the night, I bundled Michael up and walked out. I had no idea where I was going. I just stumbled along the road clutching my baby's hand. The whole of Brunei seemed to have fallen silent around us, no traffic, no people, no music.

I heard the sound of the car engine coming up slowly behind me.

'Come back,' Paul pleaded through the car window. 'You'll get into trouble with the police wandering around in the middle of the night.'

'I don't care!'

But I had no idea where I was going or who I could turn to. If it had just been me I probably would have kept walking until I got to a friend's house, but I had to think of Michael. As I calmed down I realised it was hardly fair to drag him out of his bed onto the streets like this. Reluctantly, I climbed into the car and allowed Paul to drive us home. Michael snuggled straight back down to sleep, hardly having woken up properly at all, and Paul and I talked. We talked round and round and round but I could never get him to give me any proper answers. Maybe he didn't have any.

Eventually we went to sleep, with me lying on the floor beside the bed. I decided not to leave yet. I was in a state of shock, hoping I'd eventually know what to do. Life went on around me over the following weeks as I lived in a daze. Paul changed jobs again, working in one of the royal hospitals. This job went with another massive five-bedroom house, near to the palace, so we moved yet again. The move gave me something to think about and meant we had a bit more space to get away from one another when he was at home. It was a lovely neighbourhood, full of rich and successful people, and I tried to enjoy living there, even though I was going through life like a sleepwalker. All the time I was trying to find out what was going on between Paul and the other woman, but I couldn't get any answers out of him.

Having Michael had made me think a lot about Dailyn and seeing him develop every day reminded me how much of her life I'd already missed. I wanted desperately to see her again, to let her know I hadn't deserted her and was thinking about her. On one of my trips to the Philippines without Paul, I contacted Jun and asked permission to take Dailyn out on her birthday. I wanted to introduce her to her new brother.

Jun was very friendly but told me it would be up to his parents because Dailyn was living with them. His parents weren't happy with the idea but, to my surprise, they agreed. My mother also tried to dissuade me from going, telling me it was better to cut the ties and forget, but I couldn't do it. I think they were fearful I would be hurt all over again, but I was hurting all the time when I thought about Dailyn anyway.

My brother, Christopher, had a motorised tricycle at the time and he agreed to drive me and Michael on the two-hour journey to Jun's parents' house. It was the start of a long and difficult day. Even though it had been five years since Jun and I had split up and I'd last seen Dailyn, the moment we were reunited it felt like we'd never been apart. The family had told her I'd been killed in an air crash, but I don't think she can have been old enough to take the information in, because she didn't seem at all surprised to be seeing me rising from the dead. She immediately started calling me 'Mama'. She was five or six years old by then and looked very much like I did at her age. She and Michael played as naturally together as if they had always known one another.

'Can I take her shopping in Sorsogon?' I asked Jun.

'As long as I can come too,' Jun said, glancing uneasily at his parents. 'And you must leave your passport here with my parents, to make sure you don't try to run away with her.'

I didn't argue, even though I was hurt that he thought I would do something like that. However, I could understand he had no reason to trust me after the way I'd behaved to him and I was willing to do anything if I could just spend a few hours with my daughter.

Jun drove Christopher, my two kids and me to the
city. To passers-by we must have looked like a normal little family going on a day out together. If only that could
have been true!

'It would be so nice for Dailyn to meet her other
grandparents,' I suggested once we'd bought a few things
at the market. I wanted to make our time together last as
long as possible.

'Okay,' Jun nodded, after a moment's thought. 'Let's
take her to see them.'

He agreed to drive us so we climbed back into the
sidecar and set off on the long trip to my parents' house
in Panlayaan. It was so strange to be sitting with three
people who meant so much to me. I felt very emotional
and vulnerable, but at the same time it seemed so easy.
A knot of excitement was tightening in my stomach at
the thought of how surprised and delighted my mother
would be to see Dailyn after so long.

When we finally arrived, dusty and tired, I was
shocked by how cool my mother's reaction was to
Dailyn. She didn't seem pleased to see her and made no
attempt to cuddle her. Maybe, I reasoned to myself, she
didn't want to bond too tightly, knowing they would
soon have to part again and wanting to spare both of
them as much pain as possible. Or maybe it was just too
much of a surprise and I hadn't given her time to prepare herself. She'd always told me to forget about Dailyn
because I would be able to have more kids, so perhaps

she found it easier to pretend Dailyn didn't exist. Whatever her reasons, it made me cry to see how she cuddled Michael in front of his sister.

Dad's reaction was even worse. He hadn't realised I'd gone against his advice and when he saw Jun standing outside his house he went mad, shouting at him to stay away from me. I guess he was frightened I was planning to mess up my marriage to Paul. Everyone in the family knew how much I'd loved Jun and they must all have been worried I would be tipped back into the madness that had consumed me after Dailyn's birth. Dad was ranting and raving about what people would think if they saw me with Jun while my husband wasn't there. I suppose he was already disillusioned with me because of the bar work and feared I was endangering my reputation yet again, just when I had become a respectable married woman and mother.

'You're not coming in here,' Dad shouted at Jun from the doorway to the house as Jun stood awkwardly beside the tricycle.

'It was my fault, Daddy,' I said, trying to calm the situation for the children's sake. 'I asked him to come with me. He's let me see Dailyn for her birthday, even though his parents didn't want me to.'

'His parents were right. You should listen to the advice of your elders. If you care about Jun you can go too,' Dad said. 'You can take everything you've given us and just go!'

'It's all in the past now, Daddy,' I pleaded. 'Jun has always been respectful towards you. He doesn't deserve to be treated like this.'

Angry and hurt by this reception, Jun drove to my uncle's house, about a kilometre away, and started getting really drunk. Unable to calm our father down or get any response from our mother beyond a stern look, Boy and I walked across with the children to find him.

'I'm so sorry,' I said when we got there and I saw the pain on Jun's face.

'It's okay,' he replied, trying to smile. 'It just hurts to be treated like that when I've done nothing wrong.'

Jun had hardly changed at all in the years we'd been apart. Despite everything that had happened between us I still had the strongest feelings for him. Seeing him brought back memories of the excitement of our first meetings. If it hadn't been for Paul I would probably have got back together with Jun, and now that things were going wrong with Paul I wished I could turn the clock back. Jun too was married now and talked openly about his wife. They had three children of their own, and one of the reasons Dailyn stayed with her grandparents was because Jun's new wife treated her badly. He confided that he wasn't happy in the marriage.

'My wife has dreams about you,' he told me. 'They make her wake up mad with me.'

We had hardly any time with my family before we had to start the long journey back to Jun parent's house, but it was long enough for Jun to have become really drunk. He was crying, hurt by the way my father had reacted to him, having always believed he'd acted honourably towards us.

It felt as if I'd spent the whole day bumping along in a sidecar, clinging desperately to my children, trying to make the time go slow and wanting to remember every tiny thing about Dailyn before I had to hand her back.

'Mama, can I come home with you?' Dailyn asked when the time came to say goodbye.

'I'm sorry,' I said, frightened my heart would break and I wouldn't be able to find the strength to walk away from her. 'I wish I could take you with me, but I can't. You have to stay with your grandma and grandpa.'

The rest of the stay with my parents did not go well. They were both so angry with me for bringing Jun back into their lives, and they were not getting on well with each other either, always arguing. They kept making me take one of my brothers with me whenever I went out, in case I tried to see Jun again.

Beth and Josie, having moved back from Manila, had also built a house for their family next door to my parents' stone house, which I thought would make them all happy. But now I discovered Mum and Beth had been arguing as well, with Mum saying bad things about Josie behind their backs. One day, when I came back from visiting Beth, just a few steps away from my parents' house, I found my mother crying.

'It's up to you if you want to believe what your sister tells you,' she sobbed.

All I had ever wanted was for my family to be happy.

Leaving Michael with Mum, I went into Sorsogon a few days later on my own to confirm my ticket back to Brunei, having persuaded my brothers I really did not need chaperoning. Not wanting to go home I wandered about the streets a bit and had a few drinks. It was lucky I didn't have any of my family with me because I ran into Jun. He was looking as sad as I felt.

'Can I talk to you?' he asked.

'Yeah,' I said. 'I'd like to talk to you as well.'

He drove us down to the beach. He had three big bottles of beer with him and I had a bottle of gin. We found a little beach cottage to sit in, looking out at the perfect blue sea and white sand, overhung with palm trees.

'I'm not very happy,' he confessed. 'I'm still missing you. I've always loved you.'

'It's the same for me,' I said. 'But it's too late to do anything about it now.'

'Can I kiss you?'

'If you want.'

As we kissed it was like nothing had changed. He wanted to go further but I knew it had to stop there. I was already feeling guilty for having let him kiss me. He seemed to accept it and we went back to talking. He wanted to know more about whether I was happy.

I nodded. 'Yes, I'm okay.'

He must have known from the crack in my voice and the tears in my eyes, that I wasn't being honest, but I averted my gaze to avoid more questions. I didn't want him to know just how much I was struggling in my new marriage.

'Did you ever think of taking your revenge on me for what I did to you?' I asked, eager to change the subject.

'Only once, in the beginning.'

'Do you have a knife on you?' I asked, knowing that he always carried one for self-defence.

'Yes,' he said, taking it out of his pocket.

'Give it to me,' I said. 'I'll look after it.'

He didn't hesitate, even after what I'd done to him before, and handed the knife over. It was as if he didn't care what happened to him any more.

'Are you happy?' he asked again.

'No, not really,' I admitted.

'Couldn't we get back together?'

'I don't want to think about it,' I said. I desperately wanted to follow my heart but I knew it would be terribly wrong. I owed it to Michael to try to make my marriage to his father work.

As the afternoon wore on and the heat built up I became very drunk. We didn't leave the beach until it started to get dark. I asked Jun to drop me a short distance from our house so I could walk the last bit. The moment I walked in the door my father started shouting at me, wanting to know where I'd been, as if I was still a little child who had to be in by curfew. My head was spinning and I couldn't be bothered to answer, so I just wove my way straight to my bedroom, leaving him spluttering in the kitchen. The next day, when I'd sobered up, I realised I still had Jun's knife. I asked my brothers to take me back into Sorsogon in the jeepney. We found Jun and gave him back the knife.

'Can you lend me some money?' he asked as we were saying goodbye. 'I owe your auntie's daughter.'

I gave him the money but I later discovered there was no debt, he just needed it to buy alcohol.

'You've changed,' he said, as he put the money into his pocket.

'In what way?'

'You never used to use lipstick. Why do you wear that stuff?'

I guessed he was wanting to ask if the rumours were true about me having been a bar girl in Manila, but didn't quite have the courage to ask.

'I started using it when I was working. I became independent in Manila,' I said. 'Maybe that's one of the reasons I didn't want to get back with you when you asked in that letter. And now I'm married and it's completely impossible.'

'Would you come to meet my wife?' he asked. 'She'd like to meet you.'

'I thought she was jealous of me.'

'She is, but she still wants to meet you.'

'I've been receiving anonymous letters in Panlayaan,' I said, 'saying things that aren't very nice. Could she be the one sending them?

'It's possible.'

The letters had been full of accusations, not only that I'd been working as a bar girl, but that I'd also pretended to be mad and had attacked Jun deliberately.

'Did you think I attacked you on purpose?' I asked.

'I've never ever thought that.'

I didn't want to meet his wife. I knew now what his whole family thought of me and I just wanted to get away. After that I tried writing to Dailyn on her birthdays and at Christmas, sending money in the cards, but I never heard back.

I brought Beth over from the Philippines to stay with me in Brunei, to give her a break and to give me someone to talk to. Once he saw I had company, Paul decided he could go on going out with friends, never coming back when he said he would. There was always a reason why he couldn't come home, sometimes for a few days at a time. Often he'd turn up just long enough to leave his washing for me to do, before disappearing out the door again. I said nothing, just waiting and watching, hoping that soon things would change and I would know what to do. Eventually, when he told me one more time he was about to go away on business, I couldn't repress my anger any longer. I was in his office and I wrecked everything; hurling things at the walls, tearing things up, sweeping things off surfaces onto the floor.

'You're not treating me as your maid any longer!' I screamed. 'You will respect me as I respect you.'

He left anyway, nothing changing.

The next time he came back he immediately announced he was going out with the band. This time I managed to argue calmly and it was him who lost his temper, punching me in front of Beth and Michael. I kicked him, catching him off balance and making him fall. He pulled himself back to his feet and punched me back before storming out, leaving us all crying.

We knew where the band was playing so, once I'd recovered my composure, I decided we should go up and watch them. When we got there he just ignored us. I waved to him and beckoned him over and he looked straight through me as if I wasn't there. Humiliated in front of his friends, I took Beth and Michael home and told my sister I was going to go back to try to talk to him. But once I was in the car I couldn't face it. I needed time alone to gather my thoughts, so I parked near to the shops, which were all closed and dark for the night. I felt so tired. I reclined the driving seat and closed my eyes, trying to escape from my unhappiness for just a few minutes, hoping that sleep would make things feel better. By this time it was about one in the morning.

I was dozing in and out of sleep when a knock on the window made me jump. I looked up to see two plain-clothes policemen peering in, holding up their ID cards. I tried to ignore them, hoping they'd go away, frightened of what would happen if I talked to them. But they kept knocking and calling to me. There was no choice but to open the door.

'What are you doing here?' they asked.

'I just had a row with my husband.'

They were obviously worried I was a prostitute or something, so I showed them a picture of me with Paul and Michael. They told me I couldn't stay there and offered to follow me home to make sure I was okay.

'If you have any problems let us know,' they said as they left me at the gate.

I thanked them politely and went back into the house. Nothing seemed to make sense in my head, muddled as it was by lack of sleep and too much alcohol. I was frightened now that my picture would end up on the front page of the newspapers, being brought home by the police. But all that had happened that evening really was that I'd discovered I couldn't escape that easily.

Soon after we moved into the new house our neighbour came to the door to introduce himself. He was a local Brunei man called Mr Hajji, very polite and friendly. He must have overheard something happening because at our next meeting he asked if I was happy with my husband. I told him I was, but I have never been a very convincing liar so he probably knew it wasn't true. He invited me round for a meal while Paul was away on one of his trips. I thought it would be nice to meet some new people and I asked Beth if she would come with me.

'What will I do if they speak English to me?' she wanted to know. 'I'll struggle.'

I managed to persuade her to overcome her shyness and we had a nice meal with him and his family. He then asked me to go for a meal with him on my own in a restaurant. I was very reluctant and wanted to take Beth with me again. I even told Paul about the invitation, but he didn't seem too bothered. It may have been because the man was very unattractive and Paul didn't see him as any sort of threat.

At the meal Mr Hajji told me he knew I was unhappy and he wanted to do something to help. He asked me to marry him.

'But I have a husband and you have a wife!' I protested.

'In my religion,' he explained, 'I'm allowed to have as many wives as I'm able to support. I've already asked my wife if I can marry you.'

'What did she say?'

'She just cried, but she doesn't have a choice. If she refuses she will go to hell, but if she agrees she will go to heaven.'

'No,' I said, 'I couldn't do something like that. Your wife was like a friend to me. She treated me so well at your house. I can't do that to her.'

'I'll give you whatever you want,' he persisted. 'I can build you a house. I can make your family rich.'

Although there was never any way I would have considered taking him up on his offer, it was still nice to be asked at a time when I was feeling so low about myself. I'd always thought that once I fell in love and married someone I would stay with them for the rest of my life and no one would come between us. I didn't like this idea of married men all looking around for something better.

My suitor had made his money buying and selling things, and one of those things was alcohol. He was always pressing me to take a bottle of this or that and sometimes I would give in and take them, just to shut him up. But I never felt comfortable about accepting gifts, fearful I might eventually have to give him something in return. Beth and I managed to have some fun moments, like racing him in his car on the way to work in the morning. I would be in the BMW or my Suzuki and he would be in his big high jeep, looking down at us. Beth was always urging me on to race with other cars on the roads, like we were still just a couple of kids. It all provided some temporary distraction from the unhappiness that lay beneath everything in my life, as I became more and more convinced Paul was being regularly unfaithful to me.

Eventually I wore Paul down with my questioning and he admitted he was having sex with other women. Even though I'd suspected it for a long time, having it confirmed was the most devastating blow. It felt as if my whole life had ended in a split second, but to him it seemed like an unimportant detail. During one of our arguments he even suggested I should do the same, so that we would be equal, but I think he only said it because he knew I never would, certainly not with Mr Hajji.

One day one of Paul's friends, who I had finally confided in, suggested a way to make Paul jealous in the hope that he would then realise how much he loved me.

'Buy a packet of condoms,' he said, 'and throw one of them away, leaving the empty packet so it'll look as if you've used it.'

In the confused state I was in, willing to try anything to make things better, it sounded like a good idea to me. I did exactly as he told me. Paul saw the packet but wasn't bothered at all.

When Beth returned to the Philippines I went with her, taking Michael with me. I stayed a month and by the time I came back to Brunei Paul had left his job and moved house again, away from the amorous neighbour.

Paul was now working for himself with a security alarm business. We weren't living in such a nice area as before. It was only after we'd been at the house a while that we read about a court case in the paper and discovered the address had been used by prostitutes in the past.

We were burgled one day while we were out staying with friends. I lost most of the jewellery and nice things that I'd built up since coming to Brunei. Some of it I'd bought when I was working and some I'd inherited from Jane. We had been talking about getting it insured but hadn't got round to it. When we added up what we'd lost we found it came to more than £60,000.

I was terrified the burglars would come back again and one night I heard footsteps going round the house while we were in bed. From then on, whenever Paul was away Michael and I would sleep under the bed together, with me urging him to keep quiet and not make any noise that might give away where we were. Even though I'd moved so far from my roots in the mountains, the world still seemed a big and frightening place at times, filled with predators lurking in the dark.

The arguments between Paul and I went on and on and each time they ended with me or Michael getting beaten. I often had to go and see Dr Reynolds with different cuts and bruises. He was sympathetic because he knew Paul well and understood exactly what he was like. Even though he was a friend of Paul's, I knew I could trust him to help me if things became too bad. Occasionally he would say things that suggested he thought I should do something about my situation, but he was very discreet and didn't want to push me into anything I wasn't ready for. Maybe he had come across women in my position before and knew that I would have to wait until the time was right before finally leaving.

After one particularly vicious fight, after Paul beat Michael for breaking the DVD, I went back home to the Philippines, staying with my parents again. I took Michael with me and enrolled him in a local private catholic school. This time I didn't intend to go back.

I didn't tell my family anything about my problems, allowing them to assume I had just come home for a vacation while Paul was away working. I made up stories about how Michael and I had ended up with the marks we were unable to hide, telling them we had fallen over or bumped into doors.

After a month of no communication at all, Paul came over to visit us.

'I want you back,' he told me as soon as he had got me on my own. 'Please forgive me for what I've done to you.'

By that time I was just numb and I can't remember whether I believed him or not, but when I was washing his clothes the next day I came across a half-empty packet of condoms in his pocket and I knew nothing had changed. It made me so angry that he was still cheating on me and lying to me that I found it impossible to sleep beside him in the bed. The nights were hot and I turned the electric fan on really high, partly to cool myself and partly to drive him out of the room. It seems strange to think it now, but Paul's cheating always seemed more of a problem than the beatings he gave me. I think it was because I never really knew the truth of what was going on, so I was left feeling anxious and uncertain as well as hurt.

'I can't sleep with this racket,' he complained.

'Can't you?' I asked, turning it up another notch.

He stamped out of the house and went to sleep in the jeepney I'd bought for my brother. It was called 'British Boy' after Michael. As I lay there I could hear Paul outside the window slapping at the mosquitoes as they attacked him. In the morning my father was horrified to hear I'd made my husband do such a thing. Part of me yearned to tell my parents what was going on and to make them see that Paul wasn't the wonderful son-in-law they believed him to be, but the other part of me didn't want to load them down with my problems. They had enough troubles and worries in their lives without me adding to them again. So I just kept going, with the anger bottled up inside and so many words left unspoken.

Unable to think of an excuse to give to my family without telling them the whole story, and wanting to believe he really had turned over a new leaf, I flew back to Brunei as Paul had asked me. But now I was so paranoid I was looking for trouble at every opportunity. I went through his address book and all his papers, and dipped into his emails. Everywhere I went I found evidence of other women he'd been having relationships with all over South East Asia. It seemed he just wasn't able to resist Asian women. When I came across a list of women and their phone numbers I started ringing each one to find out who they were, but I gave up halfway through. When I confronted him with the list he simply laughed and said he kept it in case I ever left him.

'I wouldn't want to be on my own,' he said, 'so I could contact one of them for company.'

On another day he left his mobile at home and when I answered a call on it there was another woman ringing from Thailand who told me she was his girlfriend.

Yet again I confronted him, begging him to tell me the truth. I guess I was driving him mad with my constant questions and my refusal to give in and let him do what he wanted. His temper snapped and he threw me down on the bed, grabbing me round the throat, squeezing with all his strength, as he shouted at me. I lashed out with my foot, catching him between the legs, forcing him to jump back and release me. We both lay there, gasping for breath, hopelessly miserable.

'What is it you want from a husband?' he wanted to know. 'Look at your life. Look at everything you have. Who provides it all? Without me you would have nothing. You know I love you, that you're my baby. I'll always be there for you.'

He didn't seem able to see how much he was hurting me and Michael. From that moment I never did any of the things he expected of a wife; no washing, no ironing, no cooking and no cleaning. I just looked after myself and Michael, eating in restaurants most of the time. Now I deeply hated Paul for the way he was treating me and his son, but I so much wanted to be part of a family, not a woman bringing up a child on her own. The easiest way to escape from my sadness was to drink. Many times I kept going until I collapsed, and Dr Reynolds often had to come and dress the wounds I inflicted on myself as I fell. I smoked all the time to try to calm my shaking. With every visit the doctor looked more concerned.

Realising things were going badly wrong, Dr Reynolds invited me up to his house for a chat, opening a bottle of wine when I got there to make the meeting more relaxed and informal. He was a gentle giant of a man, even taller than Paul at six feet four. He had told me in the past he was divorced with two grown-up children but I could never imagine him getting married again, although it would be a lucky girl who managed to catch him.

The moment I started to talk about all my problems I couldn't stop the tears. They flowed like a river as I sobbed my way through the whole story. He listened quietly, nodding his understanding and encouraging me to go on until I was left drained.

'I don't know what to do any more,' I said. 'I love Paul but I don't know what to do.'

'It's difficult,' he replied, sipping thoughtfully at his wine. 'Paul is a good friend but he's not a good husband. The only advice I can give you is to stay away from him. Move on with Michael.'

'But I've been through so much to get to this stage,' I said. 'If I walk away from him I've lost everything. I'll be on my own.'

'You won't be on your own, Gina. You have your family and a lot of friends. Any help I can give you I will.'

All I wanted was for things to be as they had been before, as if nothing had happened, but I was beginning to accept this could never be. When I got back home Paul, knowing I had been to see Dr Reynolds, was full of apologies and promises that he would never hurt me again, but I'd heard it a hundred times and every time he went back on his word.

'Why don't you write it all down in a letter to me,' I said. 'Then when you forget and go back to your old ways I can show it to you and remind you of all your promises.'

To my surprise he agreed and wrote two pages, apologising for everything and asking me to give him another chance. I was glad to have it in writing, but I still didn't believe he would be true to his word.

I'd always wondered why his friends were so off-hand with me, and it was only at this time, when I was in conversation with Edel, one of his friend's girlfriends, that she asked me if it was true what Paul said about me. Her partner, Rob, was in the band with Paul.

'What does he say?' I asked.

'That you're always arguing about money, and that you're madly jealous and insecure.'

'We've never argued about money,' I told her, 'and sometimes I am jealous but I have good cause.'

I gave her the letter that he'd signed and watched

silently as she read through it, her mouth hanging open. When she eventually looked up she was crying.

'I wish I'd known this before,' she said. 'I can't believe how much he's lied to us about you.'

'He lies all the time,' I said. 'I keep trusting him and giving him one last chance and every time he lets me down.'

From that moment on Rob and Edel became good friends to me.

Although I felt I would never recover from the hurt Paul had inflicted on me, when he said he thought we should move back to England I thought there might be a chance we could start again, away from the temptations of the expatriate life, away from other Asian women. I agreed to go. We had a car boot sale to get rid of all the possessions we didn't want to take with us, to rid ourselves of the life that had made us both so unhappy.

I knew things would never be the same as they had been when we first met, but perhaps in a different country we could build something new, for Michael's sake.

CHAPTER ELEVEN

'Mahal Kita'

We flew into Manchester airport in 2000. Even though it was still summer in England the skies were grey most of the time. I never seemed to be able to get warm away from the heat and sunshine of Brunei and the Philippines. The dullness of the weather seeped into everything. We were going to stay with my brother-in-law, David, while Paul sorted out a house and a new job. He never seemed to have any trouble finding work, so I wasn't worried about that side of things. We didn't have a car so we had to travel everywhere by train; everything was a struggle with Michael and our luggage.

David lived alone in a two-bedroom, detached village house in the Wirral part of Merseyside and was very welcoming. I always found him easy to get on with, just as if he was my own brother. He didn't have a job so he was around the house all the time, living the typical bachelor lifestyle, and was probably quite glad of the company to start with. His house was quite messy, but I was used to cleaning up after other people and it gave me something to do on the long days indoors.

I think their mother must have looked after David a lot when she was alive, now she was gone there was only Paul and me. I cleaned the house for him and did things like replacing his socks and underclothes, which had all seen better days. Paul had a tendency of talking to his brother as if he was still a little kid, which David didn't like. Occasionally David would flare up at him.

'This is my house,' he would protest, when Paul got on at him too much. 'If you don't like it you can go somewhere else.'

The moment we landed in England I felt trapped. All the friends I'd had in Brunei had gone, and my family were now a long-haul flight away. I missed the feeling of closeness that I'd had to everyone, even in Brunei. Getting home to the Philippines from Brunei had never been a problem, the flight was only a couple of hours and cost a couple of hundred pounds. Getting home from England was another matter altogether, especially the cost. My sister, Sonia, used to tell me I was lucky that I could travel the world, but I would have happily changed places with her. I was on the other side of the earth in a cold, damp country where I could hardly make myself understood because of my accent and where most of the food was a mystery to me. It was hard to even find a big enough bag of rice in the shops to feed myself for a day. Even phone calls had become an extravagance. But, I kept telling myself, it would all be worth it if Paul and I could be like we had been at the beginning of our relationship. I just needed to give myself time to adjust.

Paul had promised over and over again that his behaviour was going to change towards me and Michael, and there were times, when he was being kind, when I believed him. But then he would give one of us a look or a sharp word and I would feel a stab of fear. In my heart I didn't believe he was capable of changing and if things went wrong in England I didn't know who I would be able to turn to for help and shelter. If it was the only chance we had of getting back to how we had been at the beginning I wanted to do it, but I knew it was a big gamble and that was frightening.

Paul had a plan to import furniture and ornaments from South-East Asia and sell them on market stalls in England. I dare say he hoped that would give him plenty of excuses to go back to countries like Thailand to buy more stock. At the same time he'd been trying to get a full-time job and started going to college to improve his qualifications, so he could compete with the younger men coming up in his profession.

Our lifestyle was completely different in England to Brunei. Over there he'd earned good money and we'd lived in an economy where most things were cheap and plentiful. In England he was earning virtually nothing and everything was expensive and difficult. In Brunei at least the sun had shone on us most days, in England there was only cloud and drizzle. To pass the time I learnt to do cross-stitch, like an old lady. The pressures were building up inside my head as my needle flew in and out of the holes of my tapestry.

They must also have been building inside Paul's head. I guess he was worried about our future and the instability of our situation, even if he told me he wasn't. Everything about me and Michael seemed to annoy him, and all too often the annoyance spilled over into flare-ups of bad temper. I didn't mind it so much when he hit me, because I was always willing to hit him back and sometimes I even came off the better, but Michael couldn't do anything to protect himself, and hadn't done anything to deserve such treatment in the first place. He always looked so frightened and puzzled when his father shouted at him, as if trying to work out what it was he had to do to please him.

One day I started shaking and I couldn't stop. It was as if I'd lost control of part of my brain. I felt like I couldn't breathe. It reminded me of how I'd felt after Dailyn's birth, which made me even more anxious and frightened. I overheard Paul and David talking about me.

'I feel sorry for Gina,' Paul was saying during one of the times when he was calm and concerned about the state he could see I was getting into. 'She's not well at all and it's all my fault.'

'She'll be okay,' David tried to reassure him, without sounding convinced.

Even though I didn't like being so far from home, I did at least feel that Paul and I stood a chance of starting again, away from all the temptations of easy money and plentiful young women. Part of me had relaxed a little when it came to worrying about what Paul might be up to when I wasn't with him. But I guess I must still have had a grain of suspicion left at the back of my mind, because one day, while he was out of the house, I went into his email account using a password I'd secretly memorised while watching him working on screen, in order to check up on him.

I found some emails from Brian in Brunei saying how much he was missing Paul and remembering all the things they used to get up to together with the girls. This reminder of my past pain stoked up my anger and I emailed straight back without thinking. If he was missing his precious friend so much, I said, why didn't he invite him back to Brunei? I wrote how I knew Paul's friends had all hated me. Brian didn't come back to me.

'I want to go home,' I told Paul one evening.

'You can't just go back whenever you feel like it,' he said. 'We're here now, you've got to give it a go.'

I didn't argue because I didn't want to anger him unnecessarily.

After a few months Paul got a job working for AMEC, the giant construction and engineering company, and we decided to move to Guisborough, a town on the very northernmost tip of the Yorkshire moors, leaving David in peace. Paul assured me that once we had a house of our own again I would feel okay, that part of the pressure came from having to live with someone else. I wasn't so sure, I suspected that having David around had helped to keep things relatively calm between us, but I didn't feel strong enough to argue any more. We had to move to the area in order to look for a house to rent, so we booked into a pub called The Fox and Hounds while we looked to see what was available. At least Paul had bought a car, so we could travel around in more comfort.

Living in one room in a pub my state of mind grew worse. I was increasingly frightened of what might be happening to me. I was shaking and crying all the time and couldn't summon the energy to do anything, not even to take Michael to school. Wherever I went, even the communal areas of the pub, I would hear noises all around me and imagine people were attacking me. I just wanted to stay in the room the whole time, hiding away from the rest of the world. Paul was becoming exasperated, hitting and kicking me when his temper snapped, telling me how he wanted to go to Thailand to buy more things to sell in the markets and to get away from me. But in his calmer moments he could see there was something wrong, that I wasn't just being difficult. Eventually he insisted on taking me to see the doctor, even though

I was reluctant to talk to anyone. I couldn't see how talking about it to a complete stranger could help. I mustered all my courage and agreed.

'Mrs Donald,' the doctor said when we came into his surgery together, 'I'd really like to see you on your own. Do you think we could ask your husband to wait outside?'

I looked at Paul and I could see he wasn't happy at the idea of me talking to someone without him there to check what I was saying, but the doctor was obviously serious and Paul went back to the waiting room with a scowl.

'What's happening, Mrs Donald?' the doctor asked once we were alone. I immediately started crying, unable to keep the tears in any longer.

Ever since I'd arrived in England I hadn't been able to talk to anyone about how I felt. Everything had built up inside my head until it felt like it would burst. Like Dr Reynolds, this doctor seemed like someone I could trust. I didn't know where to start but he kept asking me questions and eventually it all came out.

'The reason we came to England was to refresh our relationship,' I told him, 'but now I feel I'm trapped here and I don't know what to do any more.'

'What do you mean?' he asked.

'My husband abuses me and my son.'

'What sort of abuse?'

'He gets angry and he hits us.'

We talked for a while and he seemed very sympathetic, but in the end he decided all he could do at the moment was give me tablets for depression. He warned me that they might make me feel worse for a while before they started to work. Everything seemed so black and hopeless and it was getting blacker all the time.

People have asked me why that doctor didn't contact social services on Michael's behalf. Since I had no idea that social services existed to protect children I didn't know what to expect of him. Maybe he did report it and no one acted. Maybe he thought I was imagining it because I was depressed. I'll probably never know.

'I just want to go home,' I kept telling Paul whenever he asked.

'You're not going home,' he insisted. 'So you have to find a way of sorting yourself out.'

Eventually, when he realised that kicking and slapping me wasn't going to work, he ran out of options and resorted to an exasperated silence. When David came to visit us he was shocked by the state I was in.

'Okay,' Paul said when David told him he had to do something, 'I'll take her back to the Philippines.'

I didn't say anything. I felt so ill and frightened of everything I just did what I was told. It was as if I was some animal they were going to return to the wild because they'd given up on any hope of house-training me. We drove to the airport and I was sitting on a bench with Michael, shivering, while Paul stamped around trying to organise flights for us. David was looking at me hard, as if lost in thought.

'Paul,' he said after a while, 'look at Gina. Can't you see she's in no state to travel anywhere? She's really sick.'

'Do you want to go back to the Philippines or not?' Paul asked me as if I was annoying him by continually changing my mind.

'Yes,' I said, 'I want to go home.'

'Gina, you can't,' David said, in a much kinder voice. 'You aren't well enough.'

They argued amongst themselves for a while and then Paul gave in and we all went back to the Fox and Hounds. I felt completely powerless, unable to play any part in whatever happened to me. That night, once David had gone, Paul went mad at me.

'Why don't you want to go home?' he shouted.

'I do want to,' I said. 'I want to get away from here.'

His exasperation was growing greater and greater as he tried to work out what he should do and I had no idea how to help him or what to suggest. His annoyance reached such a pitch the only way he could relieve it was by kicking me, saying he wanted to get out to and go back to Thailand on business. I could imagine all too vividly why he was really so keen to go back there, but I blocked it out of my mind.

One day, while he was out, I went onto the internet to check Paul's emails again. It was as if I was sleepwalking, just acting out of habit, not sure what I was expecting to find. When I saw there was one from Thailand my heart turned to lead. I opened it, already feeling sick. It was from the same girl as before, thanking him for sending her money, telling him she loved him, asking him when she would see him again.

I searched further and found Paul's reply, including the sentence, 'I just have to sort my wife out and then I'll be free to come to see you.'

Sort me out? I'd given up everything; my family, my friends and my homeland, in order to try to make our relationship work, and he just saw me as a problem to solve before he could get back to the woman he was in love with. It felt as if I was drowning and someone had just snatched away the last piece of wreckage I'd been clinging to.

'Are you still keeping in touch with the girl in Thailand?' I asked when he came back to the pub that evening.

'No,' he said, avoiding my eyes.

'What's this about then?' I asked, handing over a printout of the email.

He exploded, shouting and swearing and jumping to his feet.

'Come on,' he said, 'we're going out. I'm not staying cooped up here with you going on at me for another evening.'

I ran after him as he stormed down the stairs, shouting for Michael. He burst into the room where Michael was playing with the other children in the pub. He'd told me about these twins, whose mother, Julie, worked as the cook. I was so grateful to this unseen person for distracting Michael from his mother's increasing fragility.

'Come on, Michael,' Paul said, 'we're going out.'

'No,' Michael protested. 'I want to play.'

Paul grabbed him by the arm, dragging him towards the door, furious at being contradicted. I could see the look of fear in Michael's eyes at his father's anger. Paul tried to lift him but Michael was struggling and as Paul walked out Michael's head banged loudly against the doorframes. I screamed at Paul to stop and to be careful but he wasn't listening to anyone. Michael was screaming with a mixture of pain, anger and fear. Other people were coming out to see what was going on but no one dared to interfere.

By the time Paul got to the car it was Michael's screams that were making him furious and he pulled open the door, throwing him inside. He smacked him hard, trying to silence him, but he was only stoking the screams up louder. I watched in horror, unable to think what to say or what to do to make the nightmare stop.

'Get in the car!' Paul shouted at me and I did what he said, trying to cuddle and comfort Michael as Paul got behind the wheel and drove off at full speed. But Michael was inconsolable, nothing would quieten him down and I could tell the noise was making Paul more and more angry. I was frightened he would crash the car and kill us all.

After a few minutes he couldn't stand it any more. He slammed on the brakes, got out and threw open the back door. He leaned across the back seat, dragging Michael out of my arms and onto the side of the road, ignoring my pleas for him to calm down and not hurt our son.

'You'd better stop crying now!' he roared, going on and on, smacking him, making the screaming worse and worse. I felt as if every blow was landing on me and I realised at that moment, as I watched helplessly, that Paul was never going to change his ways. It didn't matter what country we moved to, he was always going to be violent. Eventually he threw a sobbing Michael back into my arms and drove us back to the pub without another word.

The next day we were due to move into our new house and David was so worried about the state I was in he said he would come with us. I was useless to them. I couldn't do anything at all. I felt as if I could hardly breathe, let alone carry anything. I just held on to Michael all day, both of us silent and obedient, fearful of upsetting the men as they worked.

The house we'd rented was a nice simple little two-bedroom terraced house, owned by a couple called Dave and Jane, in a pleasant village called Charltons, overlooking the Cleveland Hills.

We didn't have much furniture, we didn't even have a bed, so Paul decided we should go to Redcar, a place I'd never been before, to buy one. When we came back I asked David to get me a glass of whisky, or any type of alcohol, to try and stop me shaking.

It didn't take that long to get everything in. Once he felt we were settled David went home. I immediately felt like I'd been abandoned in the middle of nowhere. I could hear Paul talking to me, but I couldn't find the words to respond. I just wanted to hide inside my head. It was as if I'd lost every connection I'd ever had to the outside world. I sat and watched him, sipping my drink as he tried to make some sense out of the packing cases and suitcases.

'Come on,' he said, 'don't just watch me. Give a hand.'

'I can't,' I said, knowing my words probably made no sense to him at all.

Our new landlord came to make sure we were settling in all right, but still I couldn't find any words. I just hid in the corner of the room, leaving Paul to do all the talking.

'Let's go out for a meal or a takeaway,' Paul suggested when the landlord had gone.

'I'll just stay here,' I said, not feeling I could face stepping outside the door and seeing any more people. I couldn't even raise my eyes to look at him or Michael as I spoke.

'I'm not leaving you here on your own,' he said briskly and I could see he was now genuinely concerned about my state of mind, as well as irritated by it.

He insisted and I didn't have the strength to argue, so I trailed out behind him to the car and we drove back to the Fox and Hounds because it was the only place we really knew about in the area. We went into the bar and asked if they'd do us a takeaway. They agreed but said we'd have to wait. There was no way I could have sat in a public bar, feeling certain everyone was going to attack me, so I made Paul take me back out to the car to wait on my own. The whole world seemed such a frightening, hostile place.

When we got home we ate our meal together in the living room, sitting in front of the fireplace. Afterwards Paul wanted some fruit and rummaged around in the boxes for a sharp kitchen knife to peel an apple. All the time we were eating he was talking to me.

'This can't go on,' he said. 'I can't be here watching you every moment of the day. I have to go to work. We have to have an income.'

'I know,' I said, without looking up.

Michael was crying, probably because I was, and so Paul took him up to bed to get him out of the way. All I could do was pray Michael would do as he was told and Paul would have no reason to lose his temper. If he had, I couldn't have done anything about it; it was almost as if I'd lost the ability to move. When he came back down he poured us both glasses of wine and we sat together in the cluttered room, talking. It was nice that he was willing to talk to me about my problems, but it made me cry all the time because I didn't have any answers to his questions. I didn't understand what was going on in my head myself, so how could I explain it to anyone else? Inside I was blaming him, but I couldn't find the words any more. I'd said everything I could think of and none of it had changed anything.

'Why are you crying all the time?' he asked.

'I don't know.'

'Try and do something to get yourself together.'

'I don't know what to do.'

'You need to send Michael to school.'

I knew that was right because it had been worrying me, but I didn't seem to be able to concentrate on the problem long enough to find a solution. How could I begin to find out about schools when I was frightened to talk to anyone?

'Will you stop bloody crying,' he said, shaking my shoulder, seeming to struggle to keep his temper under control. 'I've told you I won't have another affair!'

'Why do you have to do this to me?' I asked. 'Why do I have to find out about this woman from your emails?'

There it was. I'd managed to say what was on my mind, despite the danger of sending him mad.

'That was a mistake,' he said, avoiding my eyes.

'How can it be a mistake after everything you've done to me and Michael?' I said. 'How can it be a mistake to keep doing the same thing over and over again?'

That night I wished I had the strength to simply run away from him, but I couldn't find the energy to do it. I felt so empty and hopeless. I begged Paul to let me go away with Michael and for him to just leave us alone. I longed to have just one friend to open my heart to, someone who would be able to comfort me that night. But all I had was a five-year-old who didn't understand what was going on and an angry husband threatening to kill me.

'I'll never let you go,' he said. 'You can't walk away from me now.'

I wasn't frightened about what he would do to me – how could I feel any worse? But what might he do to Michael? What would he do to my baby if I wasn't around to protect him?

He didn't answer for a while and I kept drinking, trying to get some warmth to my brain. It was growing late and he decided to go to bed, tired from his day's labours.

'Let's not bother to go upstairs,' he said, 'let's just lay the quilt out down here.'

'Okay.' I didn't care where we went, I knew I wouldn't be able to sleep.

He unrolled the quilt on the floor and I watched as he unpacked a duvet and pillows and laid it all out. He got ready for bed as I sat and stared.

'You've never really forgiven me, have you?' he said to break the silence.

'I wouldn't be here if I hadn't forgiven you,' I replied. 'It just hurts so much and I feel I'm trapped with you and with the hurt. I don't know what I'm going to do. I just want to get away from you.'

The self-control he'd been exercising all evening finally broke and he kicked my legs savagely, knocking me to the floor and then continued to kick my shoulders and head, shouting abuse at me. I didn't fight back, there didn't seem to be any point, and eventually he grew tired and told me to come to bed.

'Just tell me you've forgiven me,' he said as I lay silently beside him.

'What do you want?' I asked.

'I want to make love.'

'I can't.'

'Just forget about everything,' he said, fumbling to get my underwear off.

I tried to stop him but I was frightened of getting another beating and eventually he was able to do what he wanted while I cried as quietly as I could manage. It obviously wasn't as good as he had hoped for because he stopped before he'd finished and gave me another vicious kick.

'You're useless!' he snarled and I remembered all the times my father and mother had told me that during the years of my illness. After everything I'd done and everything I'd been through, I was still having that word thrown at me. 'You'll never forgive me, so what's the point?'

He got out of the bed, shaking with anger and throwing aside anything that got in his way.

'Why can't you just stop this stupid sulking?' he demanded.

'All I ever wanted was for you to love me and Michael,' I said.

In the end, at about five o'clock, he lay down and seemed to doze off. I lay beside him, cold, tired and empty, unable to feel any love for anything, even Michael. It was as if someone had switched off all my emotions.

I didn't care about anything any more. I just wanted the hurt to stop. I saw the knife Paul had used to peel his apple lying on a plate on the floor. It was within my reach. I stretched out and felt the handle resting in the palm of my shaking hand. I gripped it hard, barely able to breathe. He was the cause of all my pain. If I could just be rid of him then the pain would go.

'Mahal kita!' I cried as I turned towards him, which means 'I love you' in my native language.

I stabbed the knife in and out of his chest before he even saw I was holding it. He sat up with a shocked expression, looking down at the blood bubbling from the hole.

'I'm sorry!' he blurted. 'I'm sorry!'

He tried to get the knife from me, but I fought to hold onto it, frightened about what he would do to me now I'd angered him. He was too strong and managed to pull it out of my hand. I jumped off the quilt and ran across the room as he came after me. I didn't know where to go to get away. It was such a small room. I was completely trapped. As he lunged at me I grabbed his wrist and got the knife back. He hesitated for a second and then fell to the floor. Not stopping to think, just snatching the opportunity to stop him from getting up and coming after me again, I stabbed him a further three times, I think, in the stomach.

CHAPTER TWELVE

No Escape

Paul wasn't moving now but I didn't stop to check if he was still breathing.

'I'm sorry,' I sobbed, 'I loved you but I couldn't cope any more.'

I couldn't work out what I should do first. There seemed to be so many things to be taken care of, but in what order?

I went into the kitchen to wash the blood off my hands, watching it spread across the white plastic of the sink and then vanish down the drain as if it had nothing to do with a human life. The most important thing was to protect Michael from what had happened and whatever would happen next.

Walking in a daze, I went upstairs to find him. I wasn't sure exactly what had happened, but I did know I didn't want Michael to see his father lying on the floor covered in blood. He had enough bad memories to deal with as it was.

He was fast asleep as I came into the room, his face like an innocent angel on the pillow. I thought about leaving him in peace and going back downstairs to phone the police, telling them what had happened and letting them deal with everything. But then Michael would still be in the house when they arrived and he would have to see his mother being questioned and taken away in hand-cuffs. Then what would they do with him? Would they let him stay with me? I didn't think so. I thought he would be taken away by strangers and I didn't want that.

The only clear thought in my muddled brain was that I had to get him away from the house and find some-where safe for him to stay while I tried to work out what to do next.

'Michael,' I whispered, as if frightened of waking the dead, 'we've got to go.'

'Why are you crying, Mummy?' he asked as he opened his eyes. I cuddled him. He felt warm and soft with sleep.

'It's nothing,' I said, as I always did when he asked that question. Most of the time I didn't know myself why I was crying, so I certainly wouldn't have been able to explain it to a child.

'Where's Dad?' He didn't usually ask that, maybe some sixth sense told him something was wrong, that the rest of the house was too silent to contain another living person.

'He's at work,' I lied.

As we came down the stairs I covered his face so he wouldn't look into the sitting room, but I couldn't stop myself from glancing in, half afraid Paul might have come round and would now be looking for me to take his revenge. He still hadn't moved and I snatched up his briefcase and my handbag, thinking that everything I was likely to need would be in one or the other, and hurried out into the street, relieved to hear the front door slamming behind me.

I had no idea where I was going. The only route I knew was from the village to the Fox and Hounds. I put Michael into the car and got behind the wheel. He was awake now and looking at me anxiously. I sat for what seemed like an eternity, trying to think what I should do. I needed someone to look after Michael, someone who would care for him as if he was their own.

I wasn't sure if Paul was still alive or dead. I didn't want to live any more myself, but I couldn't leave Michael. I wanted to die, partly because I deserved to after what I'd just done and partly so I could go to the same place as Paul, if he was dead, and make sure he never forgot what he'd done to us. I decided I would take my own life, in the same way I'd probably taken his, and see him in hell.

In the rear view mirror I could see a fresh bruise coming up round my eye. My neck, shoulders and back ached from where his foot had landed earlier. In the dawn light I could see a matching bruise on Michael's face from where his father had banged him against the doorframe in the pub the day before. I hated Paul whenever I saw the damage he'd done to Michael's flawless young skin. I opened the briefcase and rummaged quickly through it, finding our passports and the return tickets to Brunei, which were now invalid.

I was trying to think who I could ring to help me, or who I could ask to look after Michael for me if I died or was arrested. The person who'd been kindest and most understanding was Dr Reynolds in Brunei. I had his number in my phone and I tried to ring it. It was lunchtime over there and I was pretty sure he would be around.

'Hello?' a voice said and then it was cut off. My phone told me I'd run out of talk time.

I remembered Michael talking about the cook at the Fox and Hounds, Julie, who had been so kind to him when I was hardly ever leaving the room, taking him to her house and letting him play with her children. I decided to drive over and ask her if she would take care of him now. He always liked playing with her twins, maybe he could become their brother and forget all about me and Paul. I had no idea what happened to orphans in England, but in my country they would be taken in by a relative or a friend. I just had to find the right friend.

'Baby, would you like to play with Ellie and Anthony for a bit?' I asked.

He smiled sweetly and I felt a warm rush of love for him.

It was getting cold sitting in the car so I started the engine and drove to the pub in a trance. It was closed and I couldn't raise anyone, however hard I knocked. I thought about waiting for Julie to come in to work, but I didn't think I could risk it. Getting back in I drove around, having no idea where I was going or what I was going to do next.

I arrived in the centre of town. I needed a phone card and I needed a taxi, with a driver who knew where he was going I was already lost. I found a newsagent who was open, the manager laying out the early delivery of the papers, and went in for a card, only to discover I'd come out without any money. There was no way I was going to go back to the house now, even if I could find my way there.

'Is there somewhere around here I can get a taxi?' I asked, having no idea how I would pay for it if I managed to find one.

'There's a 24-hour firm on the other side of the road,' the manager told me.

I went across and asked in the office for a taxi.

'May I use your phone?' I asked. 'My house has been burgled and I've lost my phone.'

'Yes, if you want. Do you want a taxi?'

I made a snap decision.

'Yes please, I need to go to the airport,' I said. If I could just get to Dr Reynolds he would help me.

The taxi driver was nice and friendly but obviously surprised I was going to Teeside airport at the crack of dawn with no luggage.

'Have you got any kids?' I asked after we'd been driving through the countryside for a while, the grey skies lightening above us.

'Yeah,' he laughed happily at the thought of them and shook his head slowly as if they were incorrigible but loveable.

I desperately wanted to ask him to take care of Michael and drop him off with Julie at the pub once I'd left, but my courage failed me. The wheels of my brain were racing, screeching inside my head like a toppled motorbike, desperately trying to work out the right thing to do. If I could get Michael back to Brunei with me, I thought, Dr Reynolds would be able to take him back to the Philippines where Beth or Mum would take him in. He would grow up with his cousins and uncles and aunts, feeling loved and part of a family.

My plan was to be sure Michael was safe in the arms of someone who would look after him properly, then I would surrender myself to the police. In my heart I still feared them from when I was a little girl looking at their blood-red gloves, but I knew I had to face my punishment. I might even be able to get Michael all the way to the Philippines myself before anyone discovered Paul and came looking for me.

'I'm sorry,' I said to the driver. 'I don't have any cash

on me because my house was burgled, but I can give you my watch. It's worth £700, and I have a few pieces of jewellery.'

'I'm not allowed to do that, love,' he said. 'Sorry. I can drop you somewhere. Another cab might take you where you want to go.'

He must have been able to tell how distressed I was and didn't make a fuss, just drove to a taxi rank. God knows where I was. I hoped I would have better luck with the next driver. I cuddled Michael all the way, kissing his bruises while he wiped away my tears with the palms of his little hands. This time the driver got me all the way to the airport, but he said he couldn't accept my watch and jewellery either when I owned up to having no money.

'I have an American Express card,' I said as we parked outside. 'I'll go in and try to get some money from a machine and bring it out to you.'

'All right, love,' he said, but he sounded doubtful. He probably thought he was being ripped off but he could see I was genuinely distressed about something and didn't want to risk making me any worse.

The terminal was busy with the early morning flights as we came in, and the hurrying passengers were dodging around the last of the night cleaners as they moved slowly around the concourse with giant mops, avoiding everyone's eyes. I found a cash machine but I couldn't remember my pin number as my brain spun hopelessly out of control. I spotted a shop selling phone cards and hauled poor Michael into it, but they wouldn't accept American Express for phone cards. Everything was crowding in on me, nothing working out. I was tired and confused and not sure what to do next. The only thing I seemed to be able to use the card for was to buy a ticket to Brunei.

I still had the return ticket to Brunei, although it was invalid. I showed it to the girl at the counter. She checked it and a few minutes later she said that a one-way ticket to Brunei was £3,500. She asked me how I would like to pay.

'Amex,' I said.

It felt as if everyone was looking at us while we were at the counter, but I told myself I was being paranoid.

'Any luggage?' the girl behind the desk asked.

'No,' I said. 'No luggage.'

Her well-groomed eyebrows rose a fraction of an inch but she smiled sweetly, as she had been trained to do. She directed us to the British Airways executive lounge.

'Mum,' Michael said as we went in to the calm, quiet lounge after having our boarding passes checked, 'I'm starving.'

There were a selection of biscuits and pastries laid out for early morning travellers.

'Can I have something to eat?' he asked, looking at them with wide eyes.

'If you want, baby,' I said, desperate not to draw undue attention to us.

I was trying to gather my thoughts. But it didn't matter how still I sat or how hard I concentrated, I couldn't make sense of everything that was buzzing around inside my head. I couldn't stop crying. Michael's eyelids drooped and he fell asleep beside me as I stroked his head. I wished I could do the same, but my brain wouldn't let me. To distract myself I opened Paul's briefcase again and sorted through all the papers, hoping I would find something that might help me work out what to do. Nothing that swam before my exhausted eyes made any sense.

Although I had my head buried inside the case, I was aware there was someone standing over me. After a few seconds I had no choice but to look up. I was relieved that the man looking down at me wasn't wearing a uniform; no blood-red gloves.

'Are you Mrs Donald?' he asked, very softly and politely as if worried he would frighten me away. He'd been called by the check-in staff at the airport who were alarmed by my appearance and behaviour.

'Yes.'

'Can I ask you why you are trying to leave the country?'

'I just had an argument with my husband,' I explained, almost relieved to be talking about what had happened.

'Where is your husband?'

'At work,' I lied, glancing sideways at Michael and feeling my face heating up with guilt.

'Where does he work?'

I couldn't lie any more, only cry.

'Mrs Donald,' he asked again, still gentle and polite. 'Where is your husband?'

'At home,' I said. 'I've done a terrible thing. I stabbed my husband.'

'Mrs Donald, we're going to stop the tickets because you aren't going to be flying anywhere today. Do you have any relatives in this country we could contact for you?'

'Yes,' I said, fumbling in my bag. 'This is my brother-in-law.'

I gave him David's telephone number.

'Where do you live?' he asked.

I tried to think, but the name of the village wouldn't come to me.

'It's near Guisborough,' I said. 'I think I can show it to you but I can't remember the address.'

As I was led from the airport to a waiting car I realised that the softly spoken man was a policeman in plain clothes. In a way I was relieved it was over and I didn't have to make any more decisions, but I still hadn't solved the problem of what to do with Michael. I was sure they would be hanging me for what I'd done, so I had to think of someone who could look after him once I'd gone. I cuddled him close to me in the back of the police car. He wasn't saying much, just looking around him at the insides of the car and the two men in the front seats.

I managed to direct them to the house without too much trouble, not like the poor tricycle driver in Manila who helped me find Beth's house all those years before.

'Wait here please, Mrs Donald,' one of the policemen said, taking my keys and going inside, leaving us with his colleague. He came out a few moments later and got back into the car.

'Mr Donald is dead,' he confirmed.

Hearing those words brought an ocean of guilt crashing down around my head. I knew he was a bastard but I still had no right to end his life. It felt as if the guilt was going to destroy me.

In my heart I'd known that he was dead, but in my head I'd been flirting with the idea that maybe he would have escaped, like Jun. Now I knew the truth. I was a murderess.

Everything was now out of my hands. They drove us to the police station and I was taken into an interview room with a policeman and woman. They'd seen the bruises all over my back and face from where Paul had been kicking me the night before. They didn't seem to be angry with me or blame me for what I'd done. They were being so kind I didn't know what to make of it.

'Please,' I said, 'just tie me up and hang me. Do whatever you need to do, but make sure my son is okay.'

'We don't hang people in England any more,' the policewoman said and I noticed she was dabbing tears from the corners of her eyes.

'If you're going to lock me up, please lock me up with my son,' I begged. 'Don't separate us now, after all this.'

'You have to have a solicitor,' she told me.

'I don't know anyone.'

'We'll find one then, to fight for you.'

'I don't want to fight any more.'

'You have to be defended,' she said. 'That's the law.'

'Whatever,' I said, willing to let fate do whatever it chose with me.

She was a nice woman.

'Do you have any kids?' I asked.

'Yes, I do.'

'Will you look after my son?'

'Don't worry, Mrs Donald,' she said. 'I will look after your son. You have to fill in a form for the social workers.'

I had no idea what a social worker was, but I refused to sign it, instinctively knowing that they were trying to get me to give Michael away.

As the morning wore on they offered to get me some lunch.

'What do you like to eat?' they asked.

'I'm not bothered,' I said, food being the furthest thing from my mind. 'I normally eat rice.'

They brought me some rice, and told me they'd given Michael some lunch as well.

'You have a gorgeous son,' the policewoman said.

'Thank you,' I said, forcing myself not to cry again.

After a while they did as I asked and locked Michael and me in a cell together. He was very quiet, his face pale and his eyes wide. He didn't ask any questions. Later in the afternoon a social worker came to talk to us. She was kind and understanding, but firm. She said she would take Michael with her to stay with a nice family.

'I just need you to sign the form,' she explained.

'I can't sign a form that allows you to take my son away from me,' I said, beginning to shake at the thought of being parted from him and left on my own. 'I've fought so hard for him, I can't just give him away.'

'I'm sorry, Mrs Donald,' the woman said. 'You have no choice, but I promise you he'll be going to people who will be very kind to him.'

'Don't give me away, Mummy,' Michael pleaded as he began to grasp what was going on around him. He started to cry.

'I won't,' I said, but it was a promise I was not able to keep.

Watching him walking away with the social worker, his tear-stained little face looking back, was the most painful thing that had ever happened to me. Yet again I was left on my own, separated from the people I loved the most, my soul heavy with guilt. I could do nothing but sob uncontrollably.

CHAPTER THIRTEEN

Fighting Back

I stayed in that cell for three days, begging all the time to be taken out. It reminded me of the box my father built for me in the house in the mountains; I felt trapped and lonely and frightened. I could remember looking at the box once I was better, trying to imagine what it had been like to be locked in there. Now I knew.

'Just tie me up,' I said. 'I won't run away. But don't leave me locked in here.'

The policewoman who was looking after me spent a lot of time holding my hand and trying to reassure me that everything would be all right.

'We can't do that,' she said. 'I'm sorry.'

I couldn't understand why everyone wasn't angrier with me after I'd done such a terrible thing. They were all being so kind, particularly this policewoman. I kept asking to go to the toilet, just for a change of scene, and she never became impatient with me. The room was so

small, with nothing but a bench to sit and lie on. I felt
I was going out of my mind.

'You'll be okay,' she reassured me whenever I started
to panic. 'Everything will be sorted out. You don't
deserve to be in here.'

They allowed me to phone Beth in the Philippines.
When I heard her voice I could imagine her in her
house, with all the family coming and going around her.
I felt a wave of homesickness and wished I'd never left
the village in the first place. It would have been better if
I'd stayed at Auntie's, cooking and cleaning and washing,
and never married or travelled. I could understand why
so many people, like my parents, were afraid of travel.

'I've done a terrible thing,' I confessed to her, all those
thousands of miles away. 'I've killed Paul.'

Even to me the words sounded incredible. I could
hear the shock and disbelief in her voice as she tried to
find out from me what exactly had happened. I
explained how Paul had been beating Michael and me,
until I finally couldn't take any more. It must have been
hard to take such news in when it came down a telephone line from nowhere, with no warning.

'Please,' I said, 'explain to everyone in the family.'

I could imagine the looks that would be on the faces
of my mum and dad when they heard what had happened; disbelief followed by exasperation and fury. Yet
again I'd brought trouble and disgrace to the family. I'd
never told them about my problems with Paul; as far as

they were concerned he was a model husband and provider. All they would think was that their 'useless' daughter had messed her life up again, running amok with a knife like before. I'd promised to repay them for all the trouble I'd caused with my marriage to Jun, and this was how I was doing it, by bringing further shame.

I wasn't allowed to smoke in the cells and the sudden withdrawal of nicotine was hard to bear when there were so few distractions. After a while I could think of nothing else, begging the policewoman to give me a cigarette every time she came in. 'Just one,' I pleaded, 'then you can kill me, I don't care.'

'You'll be going somewhere else soon,' she promised. 'You'll be better there. You'll be with other people and you'll be able to smoke.'

I knew she meant I would be going to a proper prison. I was glad because I thought that then there would be a chance I would meet other women I could talk to. There would be things for me to do for at least part of the day, I might even make some new friends – but the thought of having a cigarette was the greatest and most immediate attraction.

My memory of those first three days is hazy, much of it gone altogether, just like the time after Dailyn's birth. I do remember talking to a prosecution psychiatrist on the day I was moved, although I couldn't remember his name or face after that meeting, or anything that we talked about. I remember him being very kind, as if he was on my side rather than against me. I had other visitors but their names and faces were a blur, mixing in with the dreams I drifted in and out of in my fitful attempts at sleep. At one stage the policewoman slipped me a pack of cigarettes, which seemed like the best present anyone had ever given me.

Because of my poor English and because I didn't understand the system, I had no idea what was happening to me during the following months inside the prison. I feared I would be there for ever and didn't know how I would bear it. I could see no way I would ever be able to get out unless it was to be taken to the gallows. I didn't think I should get out, unless it was to be executed. I was guilty of the crime wasn't I? I was a murderer.

Sharing cells with other women and hearing them talk about their lives and their childhoods made me think back. I realised how lucky I'd been in the early years to be surrounded by a simple loving family and to have no cares or worries beyond where the next pair of flip-flops would be coming from. So many of the women I listened to had never known a time of complete happiness. They told me stories of how they were beaten by their fathers, their boyfriends and their husbands. They talked of their times on the streets and their problems with drugs. Most of them had had children taken away from them and some had no homes. Some of them told me they preferred being inside to their lives on the outside, calling prison the 'holiday camp'. At least they were warm and dry and fed in prison, and at least no one was hitting or raping them. Because they had nowhere to go, whenever they were released they were usually back with us a few days later. I couldn't understand that attitude. To me every month behind those bladed wires seemed like a year.

It was easy to get hold of drugs in the prison and it seemed to me that at least 80 per cent of the women were using them.

Inside my head I spent most of the time back at the house in the mountains, or down on the white sands of the local beaches, gazing up at palm trees and blue skies instead of bare prison walls lit by garish fluorescent lights. I remembered the sound of tropical rainstorms on the jungle leaves and the buzz of passing motorbikes and friendly voices, and tried to cut out the swearing and shouting going on all around me. Some of the women seemed to have no respect for the officers, even though most of the officers were really kind, but then they didn't have any respect for themselves either.

The first woman I shared with, who was in for a drugs offence, tried to ask me about my past and how I came to be there, but I wasn't able to talk about it without becoming emotional. It was all too painful. She had a full pack of cigarettes but only allowed me to have a few drags, which seemed mean. I soon learned you had to work to earn the money for cigarettes. They were a valuable form of currency.

Although I wouldn't talk about myself, I slowly started to make friends. I went to classes to get out of the cell, to pass some of the endless hours and to earn money for my own cigarettes. I went to art classes to learn to draw, as well as dressmaking and IT classes. I got on well with the teachers. The sewing teacher still keeps in touch with me. Every Christmas she sends me a card with a note, saying, 'I hope you're still doing your sewing, because you are very good at it.'

At first she didn't believe I'd been studying to be a fashion designer in Brunei, until I made a rag doll for a prison competition. It came second and I won £40.

I kept the doll as a reminder, even though it only brings bad memories of prison.

At the beginning, when I was amongst a group of women who had all run out of cigarettes, I asked if anyone had any teabags. Several people volunteered them. Then I asked for a Tampax. Someone had a roller and everyone watched as I used the teabags and the wrappers from the Tampax for a homemade smoke. I lit up and pretended to enjoy it. The others all wanted me to do the same for them and after a while we actually got used to the taste.

I learned that the other prisoners would always take whatever they could from one another and that it was impossible to trust anyone. It was a bit like being back with the bar girls in Manila. I kept myself to myself as much as possible, guarding my belongings, not wanting to antagonise anyone. I found the food hard to eat and existed pretty much all the time on noodles, so I was always hungry.

I had a phone card, which I used to call Michael every night before we were locked up. Each card cost £2 and I could make it last four nights, giving me enough time to save up from my canteen money for another. When one of the other girls asked to borrow my card I made her promise to replace it the next day because it was so important to me that Michael heard my voice every evening before he went to bed, but she never did. I said nothing, but I'd learnt my lesson and I didn't lend her anything again.

Sometimes I would be surprised by someone's kindness when they would lend someone else money if they ran out. In situations like prison you see the good sides of people's characters as well as the bad. When I first arrived some of the girls tried to give me a hard time, telling me how backward and poor my country was.

'There are poor people in every country,' I told them. 'My country used to be rich because of the gold treasure we had, but it was full of corruption in those days. I'm proud of where I come from because we all learn to stand on our own two feet. Our government never gives us money; we have to work hard for it. We can't just queue up at the Post Office each week for our cheques and then go off and spend the money on drugs. You're the sad girls; so don't call me poor. Without the handouts you would have nothing because you don't know how to look after yourselves.'

They were becoming angry and three of them came forward as if to grab me.

'Try me,' I said, staring them in the face, not backing away, ready to fight them just as I'd fought the bullies at school.

There was a moment's hesitation and they moved away, making faces as if I wasn't worth their time.

'Wow,' one of the other girls said once the bullies had gone, 'I didn't realise you were so tough, little girl.'

'Sometimes you have to be tough to survive,' I said.

From then on they were all nice to me.

Every week or two I would be taken in a paddy wagon to court. I hated those rides, they seemed so long and the wagon was so small and claustrophobic. The other women always seemed to have cigarettes on the trips, even though they weren't allowed and we were searched before we left.

'How do you manage to bring the cigarettes?' I asked one of them, watching enviously as she puffed away.

'You have to stick them up your fanny,' she said matter-of-factly.

I was shocked. I didn't know whether to laugh or be sick.

'Can I have a drag please?' I asked, once I'd got used to the idea.

One of the guards who took us back and forth was very sweet to me, always bringing me coffees, teas and chocolate. One day he even bought me a pack of ten cigarettes.

'You don't deserve to be here with all these bitches,' he whispered as he handed them over.

Once a month a social worker would bring Michael in to visit me. He'd tell me about his life in his foster family and his face would be so sad and serious when he looked at me I had to work hard not to burst into tears. I was so proud of him and the way he coped with the life I'd made for him. He was the love of my life and I just wanted to be with him all the time. I couldn't believe that I was in danger of being separated from him for ever, just as I was separated from Dailyn. He was only allowed to visit for about an hour at a time and I would see the minutes ticking away on the clock on the wall while I wanted to hold on to him for ever.

'Why are you in a place like this?' he asked me the first time, looking round at all the uniformed officers.

'I'm working here,' I lied, not wanting to try to explain the truth to him in front of other people, knowing he would be going away still thinking about my words without me there to calm his fears.

'Can't you get a job somewhere else?' he asked. 'So we can be together all the time.'

'Maybe soon,' I said.

When Julie, the cook at the Fox and Hounds, heard what had happened she wrote and came in to visit me.

She was so supportive. Two other girls who worked in the Fox and Hounds also came to see me. They told me they'd seen the way Paul treated Michael and they thought I shouldn't be punished just for protecting myself and my son. They arranged for me to change solicitors to someone who they knew would believe in my case. I was so grateful to them for all the trouble they went to for a virtual stranger.

'You need a proper criminal lawyer,' they told me. 'You mustn't just rely on whatever the state gives you.'

I'd never met Julie before. But Michael said she was kind, and she was my best chance.

'When you get out of here,' she said, 'you can come and stay at our house.'

It was so generous of her to help someone she didn't even know and I was very touched, but everyone was warning me to prepare myself for a long sentence, so I doubted if I would ever be taking her up on her offer.

The other women in the prison told me my prosecutor was a horrible man and that he would be out to get me, but he seemed okay to me in our interviews. When the day of the trial finally arrived I prayed for God to help me through the ordeal and allow me to be with my son again as soon as possible. I couldn't bear the thought that he might be grown up by the time I came out. There were so many unbearable thoughts I had to almost close my brain down to stop it from giving up under the strain. I was like a zombie, sleepwalking through all the procedures. Despite everything that had happened in my life, I'd always maintained the strong faith my parents had taught me and I felt that if I deserved any mercy God would show it to me.

Having bottled everything up for months, telling no one about my life in the Philippines, I suddenly felt the need to get it all out. All through the night before the trial I stayed awake, furiously writing down everything that had happened in my childhood and in Manila, everything in my life leading up to the moment when I snapped and attacked Paul. I hadn't talked about what I'd done at all inside the prison, thinking it better to keep quiet in case I said something that would endanger my chances of getting Michael back if I did manage to get out. But now, as the last hours ticked away, I let everything pour out, covering sheet after sheet with my neat, tiny writing.

When Dr Naismith, the prosecution psychiatrist, came to see me again in the morning I gave him my statement. He was the psychiatrist who had seen me on my first day in prison, although I have no memory of the meeting. I must have been in a state of shock during most of my time inside the prison. Over the months he had been endlessly patient as I told him about my life with Paul. He even offered me a translator but I said I would prefer to try and do it in English. Finally, I felt able to tell him my whole story.

'Is there any chance we could start again from my childhood?' I asked.

'Of course,' he said. He must have been relieved to think I was actually going to give him something to work with.

'I don't think it will make any difference to the case.' I said. 'I would just like you to know about me and how I came to do this terrible thing.'

The trial had come to court seven months after Paul died. The judge read everything Dr Naismith had written and listened to the lawyers. My defence lawyer told my story for me, so I didn't have to talk. Dr Reynolds flew over from Brunei to speak on my behalf after my solicitor contacted him, telling the court what I'd been through with Paul in the past. I never got a chance to speak to him personally because he had to fly straight back to Brunei, although we did talk on the phone. I was very grateful to him. The Philippine government had also offered to help in any way it could, even offering to fly my father over for the trial, but he declined, saying he was too old to travel now. It would have been wonderful if he had come, but I couldn't expect it of him. I was an adult now and I didn't want to cause him any more trouble than I already had.

At first I was nervous in the dock, not knowing exactly what was going on or what was going to happen to me. Every time I went into the courtroom I became more confused with everything. In the end I gave up trying to understand what was happening and just settled down to wait to find out the result.

★

'I've seldom come across anyone who has reached such a low ebb as you have,' the judge told me when he'd heard the full story of my past.

My lawyers were claiming I was not of sound mind and that I had committed manslaughter due to 'diminished responsibility'.

'I sentence you to three years probation,' the judge said, 'on the condition that you seek psychiatric assistance for the whole of that period.'

Probation? What did that mean? My lawyer was looking very pleased. I looked around and everyone was looking pleased apart from Paul's family, who had come to watch and I'm sure wanted to see me punished as severely as possible.

'What does that mean?' I asked my lawyer.

'It means you won't be going to prison,' he said. 'You're free to leave, but for the next three years you must see doctors to try to make you well, so you can look after your son again.'

CHAPTER FOURTEEN

A Happy Ending

Once you've been freed from jail you have to leave straight away, even if you don't have anywhere to go to. I hadn't been expecting to be freed and so I had made no arrangements. When I rang Julie to ask if I could accept her offer of a room in her house I discovered she was on holiday. She said she would come back to get me, but it was going to take her at least an hour and I wasn't allowed to wait around. In the meantime one of the other girls I'd shared a cell with phoned her boyfriend and told him to come and pick me up from the prison gates. I declined, preferring to wait for people I knew.

'You were the only one who was nice to me in here when I was depressed,' she said. 'You shared your cigarettes and opened your arms to me when I needed you.'

Everyone was being so helpful but I didn't know what was happening or where I was going to end up on my first night out. I didn't know anyone in England apart from Paul's family, and they were hardly likely to welcome me into their homes.

All I really wanted to do was find Michael and cuddle up with him, shutting out the rest of the world, but he was in his foster home and the social services wouldn't be allowing him to come back to me until they were sure I was in a position, both financially and mentally, to look after him properly.

I waited for an hour, then John, Julie's husband, arrived and we went to Redcar police station to collect some of my clothes, which were still there.

I soon realised John and Julie were a very close couple, always kissing and hugging. It was a lovely sight but it broke my heart, making me realise even more acutely just how alone I was in the world. My demons had made me attack the person I would have wanted to spend my life with and had led me to marry someone who had demons of his own. Now they had played their worst trick and left me alone, separated from both of my children. I felt totally isolated, especially when I was with John and Julie and saw how much in love they were.

As well as the twins, Julie had three children from her first marriage, so there was always plenty of bustle going on. Julie was working in a restaurant called The Rabbit and Onion and often had to work nights. I felt uncomfortable at first being left with John and the twins in the evening and I would stay in my bedroom or do some cleaning to occupy myself whenever Julie was out. The more I got to know John, however, the more like a big brother he became, despite the language barrier between us. He was a gentle man, always joking.

The social workers would bring Michael on visits, but they had to stay in the room with us all the time, watching the way we behaved together to try and work out if I was ready to be a full-time mother again. I suppose they wanted to be sure I wouldn't attack him as I'd attacked his father, but I could never have done anything to harm him, he was my only reason to go on living. I couldn't imagine I would ever want to be involved in a relationship with another man apart from Michael.

He seemed much happier now he could see I was out of prison and he told me his foster family were being nice to him. I thought that if I could just get him back we could return to the Philippines and live amongst our family. I longed to be able to hug my mother and feel safe like I had as a child, but I had no idea if that was going to be possible or how long it would take to achieve.

I stayed with John and Julie for about a month. I was so grateful to them because it was such a brave and kind thing to take someone into their house who had done the things I'd done, especially when they hardly knew me and owed me nothing. They were truly kind and self-less people. I felt guilty because I wasn't able to get any money out of my bank and had no way of paying them back for their hospitality, other than helping around the house as much as I could. Often Julie would give me £5 or £10 to go and buy sweets or cigarettes for myself.

Their neighbour, Simon, had recently broken up with his girlfriend and he started to pay me a lot of attention. Even though I hadn't imagined I would ever want to go out with another man, it was nice to have someone sympathetic to talk to. I could talk to John and Julie, but in the end they had each other and I didn't want to impose on them more than I already was. Simon calmed me down whenever things got too much and I became upset. I found myself growing close to him as a friend. He invited me round to his house one evening and we did a lot of drinking as we talked and I unburdened my soul. The next thing I remember was waking up in his bed the next morning.

'How did I get here?' I asked.

'I carried you,' Simon grinned.

'You been shagging my boarder?' John joked when the two of us went round later.

'What does shagging mean?' I asked, and they both laughed.

'You don't want to know, Gina,' John teased.

Simon leant me some money so I could contribute to the household expenses at John and Julie's and I promised to pay him back as soon as I could get access to what was left of my money from Brunei.

Julie got me a job cleaning in the local pub, The Black Swan, so I had some cash coming in. John and Pat Trenholm, the publicans, were very understanding, allowing me to work early in the morning to avoid having to face the public. Pat even organised me a house to rent.

'Gina the cleaner,' John would call me, 'and the best cleaner in Guisborough.'

Within a month of coming out of prison I'd managed to convince the social workers it was safe to let Michael come back to me. I was so happy that day that I thought I was going to float away on a cloud. I couldn't stop hugging and kissing him, frightened that if I let go for even a second I would lose him again.

Although it was wonderful to have him back it was obvious to me that when we were together there was someone missing. He never mentioned Paul, and neither did I, but I'm sure he felt his father's absence. I certainly wouldn't have wanted to have Paul back with all the fear and the violence, but I couldn't deny there was a gap in our lives now he was gone. I was also having trouble with my neighbours.

Simon popped round to the house so I could pay him back the £300 I owed him, and a neighbour saw him coming in the backdoor. The next day the social worker arrived, asking questions about who this mystery man might be.

'You're not supposed to be involved with a man,' she explained.

I managed to reassure her Simon was just a friend who'd lent me some money. On the next visit she went through my kitchen cupboards to check if I was feeding Michael enough and looking after him. Because they were giving me a few pounds a week to help support Michael until I was earning enough, they said they had the right to check what I was spending it on. I didn't want to say too much for fear they would take Michael away from me again, but I told them I would rather not have the money and be allowed to keep my privacy and dignity.

Despite the fact that some of the neighbours were watching me every hour of the day and night, I still went out with Simon when I could. I knew our relationship was never going to be more than just good friends. I felt safe when he was around, able to face the world.

On one of our nights out with John and Julie I met another man, called Nick. He was gentle and softly spoken. He had recently been divorced. As soon as we started talking it felt as if we'd known one another all our lives. It was so comfortable. There was a karaoke machine in the pub and I was singing 'One Moment In Time' and 'La Isla Bonita', having drunk enough to give myself the courage, when Nick first spotted me.

'Her voice is terrific,' he said to a friend of his. 'So strong and so much depth.'

'Don't even go there, mate,' his friend said, 'she's the one who killed her husband.'

'That didn't put me off at all,' he later told me. 'Because you were the most beautiful woman I'd ever seen. Your voice made my hair stand on end.'

I laughed at that because he was completely bald, and I liked the way he joined in the laughter.

We didn't get a chance to talk on that first night and the party ended with Simon giving me a piggyback down the street.

The next time I saw Nick I was sitting alone in a restaurant, waiting for Simon, and Nick came in with a group of friends. He was with a girl, but he seemed to forget all about her and came straight over to talk to me. He didn't drag himself away until his food was served up and his date started complaining. He said she wasn't his cup of tea anyway. Simon didn't show up, and I left the restaurant soon afterwards and went back to the Black Swan. I was sitting at the bar alone when Nick and his friends came in after their meal. He started talking to me again, but I was a bit drunk by then. Someone said something horrible to me about Paul's death and I burst into tears. Nick was horrified and tried to comfort me.

We didn't meet again for a few weeks, although Nick tells me I was on his mind all the time. His daughter, Emma, used to come and stay with him on Saturday nights, and on Sunday mornings they would come into the Black Swan to walk Bill and Ben, John and Pat's spaniels.

On one of their visits Michael opened the door to them and started chatting to Emma. Being as cheeky as always, he asked if he could go up into the hills with them.

'It's okay with me if it's okay with your mum,' Nick said, having taken a liking to him. He had no idea whose son he was.

Michael came running to find me, begging me for permission. 'Sure,' I said, always grateful to anyone who would pay Michael attention, aware that he didn't have fun with me because of my fear of going out and facing strangers. Nick still didn't realise he was my son, even when these walks became regular occurrences. It wasn't until some weeks later, when he turned up at the pub early for a trip to the races, that he saw me packing up from my cleaning shift and getting ready to go home. We immediately started talking again and he asked if he could ring me. I gave him my number and late that evening he called.

He came to the house that night, soaking wet from a rainstorm. It seemed the most normal thing in the world to give him one of my dry t-shirts and to towel his head for him. We opened a bottle of wine and chatted until I eventually fell asleep on the settee and he watched me sleeping.

'Come round to my place for Sunday lunch,' he said before he left. 'I can cook, you know.'

I thought that would be really nice. On the Sunday, just as Michael and I were setting out, I rang to check everything was okay and found he'd overslept and there was no food prepared. To make up for it he took us out for lunch and we went for a walk together afterwards. I could see Michael was as comfortable with him as I was. It felt as if the gap Paul had left had been filled.

Nick was able to read my face, always knowing if I was unhappy from the way I would stare into space. Sometimes he would just sit beside me and hold me while I cried, wiping the tears away. When he told me he loved me I was really touched but frightened I would end up in pain again.

Working as a technical writer he was always going away on jobs, but he phoned me all the time and it still felt like the most natural and comfortable relationship. Whenever he did come home we immediately felt like a family together.

At that time I still found going out in public hard and would often have panic attacks, sometimes as many as eight in a single day. Nick would take me out late at night or early in the day, when I knew there would be fewer people about, to get me out of the house. Each week we would adjust the time slightly, bringing me more into contact with the public. While most people were fine there were a few who weren't very nice, shouting abuse at me. Once, someone asked Nick if he'd bought me off the internet, and another time someone told Nick I was just a gold-digger, after his money, and I cried for days.

Although their comments upset both of us, I knew the best thing to do was to let it go in one ear and out the other. Nick kept telling me, over and over again, that I'd done nothing wrong and had nothing to feel ashamed of. He told me I should be proud of who I was and how far I had come.

'But everybody's looking at me,' I'd say.

'Don't be silly,' he'd reply, 'it's only because you're a different colour, with different hair. At least you've got hair.'

He would rub his bald head ruefully and I would laugh.

As I wasn't getting on well with my neighbours, Nick suggested Michael and I moved into his flat since he was away most of the time. It was an invitation I was happy to accept since I was now allowed to live with a man. The moment we moved in I felt safe and relaxed, Nick was so gentle, funny and romantic.

Believing we needed to get away more, he bought a caravan at Primrose Valley in Scarborough and we would take the kids there at weekends. I called myself Christine when we were there to try to avoid being recognised as 'that murderess'. I finally felt I could go out without fear, holding my head high. I was always uncomfortable about holding hands in public; it wasn't something I would have done at home in the Philippines, but Nick insisted. Whenever we passed another person he would grip me more tightly so I couldn't pull away, making me feel very secure.

One day we went walking on the beach. It was great to be beside the ocean again, even if the sea was greyer than the sea of my childhood, and the beach stonier. I saw a jellyfish stranded on the sand. Not knowing what it was I scooped it up before Nick could stop me, getting badly stung. I still had so much to learn about my new home country.

At the caravan site I learnt it was possible for us to go out as a family in public, all three of us holding hands with our heads held high. Nick took us to a magic show and we sat in the front row. He kept holding my hand, even though I knew my palm was growing clammy with sweat. But it was okay; no one said anything or looked at us strangely and I was able to relax and enjoy the show. When we got home to Guisborough Nick persuaded me to do the same there. We walked around town holding hands like teenagers, and a few weeks later we went to a nightclub. A few weeks after that I stood up in a crowded pub and sang to Nick. I could see he was crying.

'Why were you crying?' I asked when I sat down again.

'Because your singing was so beautiful.'

'No, really, why?'

'Because I can see you're back to normal.'

I won't pretend I have been able to just forget everything that has happened in my past. Nick had also suffered damage from his own experience of a broken marriage, so the early days of our relationship was plagued with all the usual ups and downs you would expect when a couple are both volatile and vulnerable. But we came through each bumpy patch closer and more aware of the needs of the other. Because we were still living in the same place there was gossip from some people, and we had to listen to a lot of racial innuendoes and slurs, but we didn't want to move unless it was to go back to the Philippines. We didn't want to feel we'd allowed other people to drive us away. We had some good friends in the area and Michael was settled in his school.

In August 2003 Nick and I got married, with Julie and John's twins as bridesmaid and pageboy. It was to be my third wedding and I was still only 29 years old. It was a sunny day but I still felt sad because, while we had a lot of friends, I knew there were still some people who had a low opinion of me. A limousine picked me up at 10.30 and drove us to the registry office in Guisborough.

'Are you excited?' Nick asked.

'I don't know,' I said, 'I think I'm just a little sad about some of the things people have said about me.'

He looked crestfallen.

'It's nothing to do with you and me,' I said quickly.

When we got out of the limousine I saw the face of someone who I knew thought badly of me, but I kept smiling, determined to be strong for Nick.

It's impossible to compare the love you feel for different people. From the moment I met Nick I felt close to him and I knew it was more than just friendship. He's the most fantastic father to Michael and no one would ever guess they weren't related by blood. They do everything together, even going fly-fishing, although I think the pair of them hook themselves more often than they hook any fish. They have also both fallen in the river and have caught nothing but sunburn and colds. It's impossible not to love someone who loves Michael that much. I only wish I could include Dailyn in the family unit as well, and when I think of how long it has been since I saw her the sadness returns. I love Nick so much, even though I find it hard to show it as much as he would like. I couldn't ask for a better partner.

It feels like I've travelled a million miles from the house in the mountains where my life started, just over 30 years ago, but at last I feel I have come home.

EPILOGUE

In March 2004, after almost five years of separation, I managed to go back to the Philippines to be reunited with my family on a five-week visit. There had been times, when I was sitting alone, staring at four walls, when I didn't think I would ever see them again. I doubted if I would ever feel the warmth of the tropical sun on my skin or see the bright turquoise seas. It had seemed like there was no light at the end of the tunnel.

To actually be cuddling the mother and father I had thought I would never see again was an indescribable joy.

At the same time it was weird to be introducing them to their new son-in-law after what I had done to Paul.

The whole family knew what had happened but everyone was crying and thanking God for my safe return.

Mum and Dad behaved as if nothing had happened and were as kind and respectful to Nick as they were to Paul.

When Nick told them he wanted to learn to climb the coconut tree, Mum showed him how, even offering him her shoulder as a climbing frame – an offer he accepted. She is 58 years old now and weighs no more than six stone.

Our five-week visit went too quickly and when we got back to England we all found ourselves feeling homesick. But this is my home now. If Dailyn could just be allowed to come and stay with us, I would have everything I could have hoped for. I wish I knew if the letters I write to her ever arrive.

ACKNOWLEDGEMENTS

I would like to thank all my friends and family, for their support.

I would like to thank Michael for giving me the courage to hold in the pain, pain that nobody could imagine unless they had been through it themselves. Thank you very much my darling son. Words are not enough for what needs to be said between us. I would like to thank Dailyn for being my beloved daughter, even though we have been separated by so many miles for so many years.

I would like to thank Mama and Papa for helping me and giving me all their moral support throughout the court case. I would like to thank them for the upbringing they gave us all, which made us strong.

Thank you to Dr Reynolds, without your help would they ever have believed me when I told them what I'd been through? You saved me from a life in prison.

Thanks to Dr Naismith for being so patient and allowing me the opportunity to open my heart and start the story from the beginning.

Thanks to Babs and Michelle, two friends from England who sent me postal orders and magazines while I was in prison.

Thanks to the foster parents Julie and Dave Lofts for looking after Michael and being there for him when I couldn't be.

Thanks to Edel and Rob for sending me some clothes.

Thanks to the Filipino priest for coming to visit me in jail, I'm sorry I can't remember your name. Thanks to the Philippine Embassy in London for the postal orders when I was in jail.

Thanks to my current bosses, Tracy and Paul from The Huntsman, for giving me a chance, you are good friends and the best bosses I could ever have.

Most of all I would like to thank John and Julie Mac and their family. You welcomed me into your home when I needed it the most and had nowhere to go. You are an amazing family and I adore you all. God bless you XX.

My special thanks to my husband, Nick. Thank you very much, darling, for giving me the courage to face the world again, without you it would be impossible to smile again. What you did for Michael and me has meant a lot to us. Although you're so often away, I know your heart is always with me.

I would like to dedicate this book to Nick and Michael. Thank you both for being there. You're both very special to me.

About the Authors

Gina French was born in the mountains of Luzon, the Philippines, in 1973. She is now happily remarried and lives in Middlesbrough, England, with her son.

Andrew Crofts is one of the UK's leading ghostwriters. His books include a string of number one bestsellers, including *The Kid, Just a Boy, Sold* and *The Little Prisoner*.